CRAFTING FUN

for Kids of All Ages

CRAFTING FUN

for Kids of All Ages

Pipe Cleaners, Paint & Pom-Poms Galore, Yarn & String & a Whole Lot More

KIM ULIANA

Sky Pony Press

NEW YORK

Sky Pony Press books may be purchased in bulk at special discounts for sales promotion, corporate gifts, fund-raising, or educational purposes. Special editions can also be created to specifications. For details, contact the Special Sales Department, Sky Pony Press, 307 West 36th Street, 11th Floor, New York, NY 10018 or info@skyhorsepublishing.com.

Sky Pony® is a registered trademark of Skyhorse Publishing, Inc.®, a Delaware corporation.

Visit our website at www.skyponypress.com.

10 9 8 7 6 5 4 3 2 1

Library of Congress Cataloging-in-Publication Data is available on file.

Cover design by Jane Sheppard
Cover photos by Kim Uliana

Print ISBN: 978-1-5107-1937-8
Ebook ISBN: 978-1-5107-1938-5

Printed in China

To my little bear, thank you for all of the inspiration. May your creativity continue to blossom. And to my big boo, thank you for loving and supporting me despite a craft supply–filled mess of a house. Love to you both.

CONTENTS

INTRODUCTION

Hi, my name is Kim and I am thrilled that you have purchased our book! The inspiration for this book is my life. I am a mother, blogger, crafter, and an artist. Art & creativity are such a huge part of my life that it was important for me to be able to share it with my child. I began doing arts and crafts with my daughter before she could even say the words "arts and crafts." Our blog, *The Pinterested Parent*, chronicles all of the arts and crafts adventures that I share with my pre-schooler. We do a combination of child-led arts and crafts and guided ones; both have grown her creativity. Experimenting with different methods and materials has expanded her artistic mind. In fact, many projects posted on our page, thepinterestedparent.com, are credited to ideas and suggestions that she offered.

The crafts shown in this book vary in skill level, but many can be simplified or kicked up a notch to suit your child's particular needs or skills; these crafts are just a guideline for ideas. Let your child put their own spin on their projects. After all, arts and crafts are all about having fun and expressing yourself! We work with a wide variety of craft supplies that you will find listed for each project, but there are some items that will commonly be used that are not listed on your materials list.

- Newspaper, drop cloth, or wax paper to protect your work area
- Scissors
- Paintbrushes
- Pencils
- Water or paper towels for cleaning paintbrushes and work area

Important

While most of the supplies listed are basic craft supplies that are used regularly by children, adult supervision is recommended. Special attention should be made when operating a glue gun, scissors, staplers, or anything that could be considered a choking hazard. Some projects may require adult assistance. Safety scissors and low-temperature glue guns are a good choice, but still require instruction and supervision. We use paints in many of our crafts. We use watercolors, tempura paint, and acrylics in most of our projects. We recommend selecting paints that are nontoxic. There are many paints that are made just for kids. If your child is prone to putting their fingers in their mouth, it is not recommended that you let them paint without proper supervision. There are many homemade edible paint recipes that can be found online and are safe for small children.

CHAPTER ONE

ALL THAT GLITTERS

Glitter, sequins, and gemstones add a special touch
and sparkle to any craft.

GLITTER MERMAID

SUPPLIES

- Construction paper
- Markers or paint
- Yarn
- School glue
- Glitter

DIRECTIONS

Cut the shape of the mermaid's tail and top out of a piece of construction paper. Glue the pieces to the middle of a piece of white construction paper. Use markers or paint to make your mermaid's body and face. Glue strands of yarn to your mermaid's head to make colorful mermaid hair. Squeeze glue onto the mermaid's tail and top and sprinkle glitter to the glue to add a little magic to your mermaid. Let the glue dry and then shake off the excess glitter.

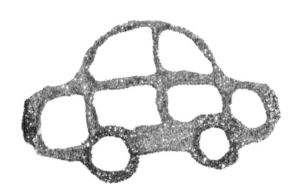

GLITTER GLUE PEELS

You can also try these with puffy paint to make window clings.

SUPPLIES

- School glue
- Wax paper
- Glitter

DIRECTIONS

Squeeze glue onto a piece of wax paper to draw a picture or to form a design. Shake glitter over the glue until it is covered. Let the glue dry; it may take a day or two before it is dry enough. Once it's completely dry, carefully peel back the dried glue from the wax paper. If you would like to display it, tie a string to it and hang it.

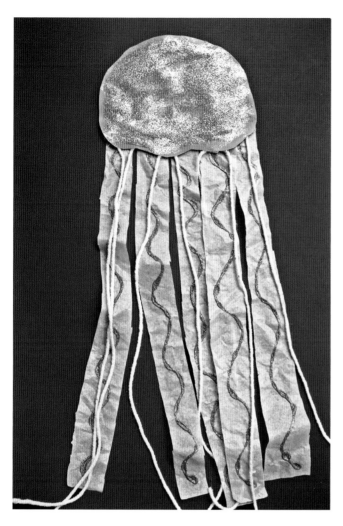

GLITTERY JELLYFISH

Jellyfish are so lovely; there is something magical about them. Accompany your craft with a little lesson about the enchanting sea creatures.

SUPPLIES

- Construction paper
- School glue
- Glitter
- White tissue paper
- Yarn

DIRECTIONS

Cut an oval shape with a wavy bottom out of a piece of construction paper. Squeeze glue out onto the shape and spread it. Shake the glitter onto the glue and let it dry. Cut long strips of white tissue paper and squeeze lines of glue all the way down them. Then shake glitter onto them and set them aside to dry. When all the glue is dried, shake off the excess glitter. Cut strips of yarn longer than the tissue paper. Glue the strips of tissue and the yarn to the back of the jellyfish's body.

CARDBOARD MAGIC WAND

This is a simple craft to make that will add a little extra magic to your pretend play.

SUPPLIES

- Cardboard
- Silver acrylic paint
- Wooden dowel
- Low-temperature glue gun
- Pipe cleaner
- Tacky glue
- Glitter

DIRECTIONS

Sketch a star shape onto a piece of cardboard and then cut it out. Paint it silver and set it aside to let it dry. Paint the wooden dowel and let it dry. Using the glue gun, glue the dowel to the star between one of the points. Wrap a pipe cleaner around it. Line the edges of the star in tacky glue and shake glitter over it to finish it off. You may add ribbon to your wand, as well.

Kim Uliana 3

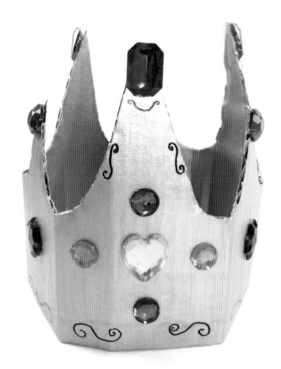

CARDBOARD JEWELED CROWN

If you have a child that loves to play dress up, this is a perfect project for them.

SUPPLIES

- Cardboard
- Gold acrylic paint
- Low-temperature glue gun
- Plastic gemstones
- Tacky glue
- Markers

DIRECTIONS

Cut a long strip of cardboard. Roughly measure how long it will need to be to fit around your head and then cut a wavy pattern across it, alternating between taller and then shorter spikes. Paint the front and back of the cardboard in gold. When it dries, bend and curve it into a ring for a minute or so to loosen it up so that it is not too rigid. It will form a better crown shape once it is loosened. Connect the crown by using a low-temperature glue gun to join the two ends together. Once the glue dries, glue on the gemstones with tacky glue or the low-temperature glue gun. Use markers to draw on designs.

DESIGN YOUR OWN NECKLACE OR EARRINGS

This is a great activity that you can use to learn about patterns or to make for fun.

SUPPLIES

- Construction paper (any color)
- Gold or silver marker
- Tacky glue
- Plastic gemstones

DIRECTIONS

Cut a simple head bust shape out of a flesh-toned piece of construction paper. Glue it down to a piece of construction paper in any color. Use a marker to draw in a chain or earring dangles. Use the gemstones to design a necklace around the neck. Form patterns or just have fun decorating your perfect necklace and earrings.

MASQUERADE MASKS

You can embellish your masks with whatever you choose. For one of our masks, we used the tiny circles left over from punching holes into construction paper with a hole punch. Use pom-poms, markers, stickers, or ribbon to add a little pizzazz to your masks.

SUPPLIES

- Cardboard
- Acrylic paint
- Tacky glue
- Plastic gemstones
- Paper circles (from hole punch)
- Glitter
- Craft sticks

DIRECTIONS

Cut a mask shape out of a piece of cardboard. Paint the cardboard in the color of your choice and set it aside to let it dry. Squeeze out and spread tacky glue all over your mask. Place and glue the embellishments of your choosing onto the cardboard. Sprinkle glitter all around. The glitter will stick to the glue on the bare portions of the mask. Glue a craft stick to the back of the mask on one side.

PAINTED ROCK & GEM PAPERWEIGHT

The rugged texture of the rocks and the smooth surface of the gemstones work nicely together. The glittery painted rocks could also work well with other crafts or for an accent in a fairy garden.

SUPPLIES

- Small rocks
- Acrylic paint
- Glitter
- Wax paper
- Air dry clay
- Rolling pin
- Round cookie cutter
- Plastic gemstones

DIRECTIONS

Collect and wash small rocks. Let them dry and then paint them in assorted colors using the acrylic paint. While the rocks are still wet, shake glitter over them and then set them on wax paper to let them dry. Grab a chunk of clay and sprinkle with a little glitter and knead it in. Roll out your clay with a rolling pin and press the cookie cutter into it to cut out the shape. Leave the clay in the cookie cutter if you want to prevent your shape from spreading while you press on it. Press gemstones and the glittery rocks into your clay. Let the clay dry for one to two days. If the gemstones loosen while drying, use tacky glue to glue them back into place.

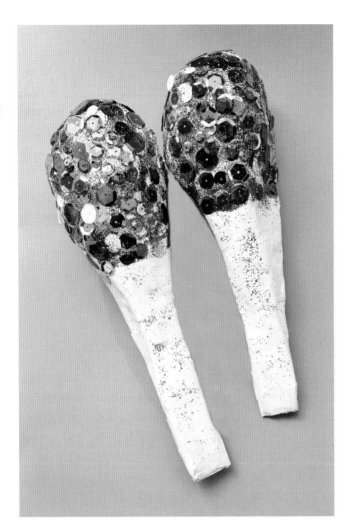

PAPIER-MÂCHÉ MARACAS

Making music has never looked so lovely. The sequins and glitter add a festive flair to these homemade percussion instruments.

SUPPLIES

- Jumbo plastic eggs
- Beans or popcorn kernels
- Jumbo craft sticks
- Newspaper
- Water
- School glue
- Acrylic paint
- Sequins
- Glitter

DIRECTIONS

Fill two jumbo eggs halfway with beans or popcorn kernels and put the tops back on. Tape two craft sticks around the bottom of each egg so that the craft sticks are hugging the egg. Tear strips of newspaper and set the strips aside. Make a mixture of water and school glue to form the papier-mâché paste. Dip the pieces of newspaper into the paste and wrap the strips around the egg and the craft sticks tightly. Smooth out bumps with your fingers as you go. Use smaller strips to fill in small creases. Continue to wrap with newspaper until you reach your desired size and shape. Do this with both eggs. Let the newspaper dry overnight. Paint your maracas in the color or colors of your choice. When the paint is dry, smooth glue all over the fattest part of the maracas and then cover in sequins and glitter.

PAPER PLATE MIRROR

What do your children see when they look in the mirror? Challenge them to use a mirror while making their portrait. The mirror also can make a great prop in fairy tale pretend play.

SUPPLIES

- Acrylic paint
- Paper plate
- Craft stick
- Tinfoil
- School glue
- Plastic gemstones

DIRECTIONS

Paint the outer ring of a paper plate in the color of your choice. Glue a craft stick to the bottom center of the plate. Cut a circle out of tinfoil large enough to fit into the center of the paper plate. Glue gemstones all around the outside edge of the tinfoil. Use acrylic paint to paint a self-portrait of yourself onto the tinfoil.

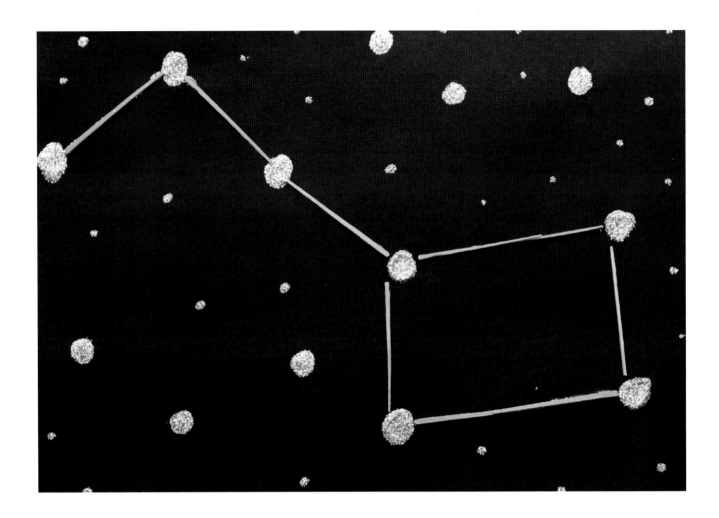

SPARKLING CONSTELLATION

This would be the perfect companion craft to some actual stargazing. Search for constellations and model your glittery constellations after your favorite ones.

SUPPLIES

- Toothpicks
- School glue
- Black paper
- Silver glitter

DIRECTIONS

Form the shape of a constellation, such as one of the dippers, using toothpicks. Glue the toothpicks onto a piece of black paper, leaving a little bit of space in between toothpicks. Squeeze circles of glue in the spaces between each toothpick and then sprinkle with glitter. Make smaller circles and dots of glue around your paper and shake on more glitter. When the glitter dries, shake off any excess.

SEQUINED LAVA LAMPS

This is a beautiful science experiment that your kids are sure to love and it's mesmerizing to watch. Ask your child their observations during the experiment.

SUPPLIES

- Clean 20-oz. plastic bottle
- Vegetable oil
- Water
- Food coloring
- Sequins
- Alka-Seltzer

DIRECTIONS

Fill a clean 20-oz. bottle about two-thirds of the way with vegetable oil. Fill the bottle up the rest of the way with water, leaving some space up top to allow for the bubbling. Add a few drops of food coloring and add the sequins. Let everything settle and then break an Alka-Seltzer tablet in half and add to the bottle. Watch your sparkly lava lamp dance! Add more tablets as needed to watch your lava lamp bubble again.

SPARKLE DRAGON

Make different colored dragons. Add a craft stick to them and make your dragons dance.

SUPPLIES

- Construction paper
- Googly eye
- School glue
- Sequins
- Glitter
- Red tissue paper

DIRECTIONS

Cut a wavy dragon shape out of any color construction paper. Glue a googly eye to the head. Make wavy lines across the dragon's body with the glue. Do one wave at a time and place sequins over the glue, alternating between glitter and sequins. Let the glue dry and then shake off any excess glitter. Cut jagged pieces of red tissue and glue to the mouth to form fire.

SEQUINED FISH

Sequins make beautiful shiny scales for these fish.

SUPPLIES

- Construction paper
- Tissue paper
- School glue
- Sequins
- Large googly eye

DIRECTIONS

Cut a fish shape without any fins out of a piece of construction paper in the color of your choice. Cut wavy strips of different colored tissue paper and glue the strips fanned out to the back end of the fish to form rear fins. Squeeze wavy lines with the glue vertically across the body of the fish. Place sequins on the glue. Glue a googly eye to the fish to finish it off.

TREASURE CHEST

You can use plain solid-colored paper for the chest, but the wooden scrapbook paper adds a nice touch.

SUPPLIES

- Wooden scrapbook paper
- Construction paper
- Black Sharpie
- School glue
- Plastic gemstones, sequins, and buttons

DIRECTIONS

Cut two rectangles out of a wood-design scrapbook paper. Make one taller than the other. Cut another rectangular shape with a rounded top. Place your pieces onto a piece of construction paper. Glue the smaller rectangle above the larger rectangle and then add the rounded piece over the small. Outline your two rectangles in black Sharpie and then draw in your lock. Glue gemstones, sequins, and buttons to the smaller rectangle. Glue some spilling out of the chest and around it, as well.

CHAPTER TWO

BUTTONS, BUTTONS, BUTTONS

Buttons are so much fun to work with! They are great to use in crafts, to add to artwork, for sensory play, and stringing them up is a wonderful way to sharpen fine motor skills.

BUTTON BEEHIVE

SUPPLIES

- Yellow, black, and blue construction paper
- School glue
- Yellow buttons
- Black marker

DIRECTIONS

Cut a wavy oval shape out of a piece of yellow construction paper and glue onto a piece of blue construction paper. Cut an oval out of a piece of black construction paper and glue it to the bottom one-third of the hive. Glue the yellow buttons all around the hive, avoiding the black oval piece. Cut two circles, one smaller than the other, out of yellow construction paper. Glue the smaller circle over the other circle to form a bee. Glue the bee or bees around the hive. Draw the stripes, face, stinger, and wings onto the bees with a black marker.

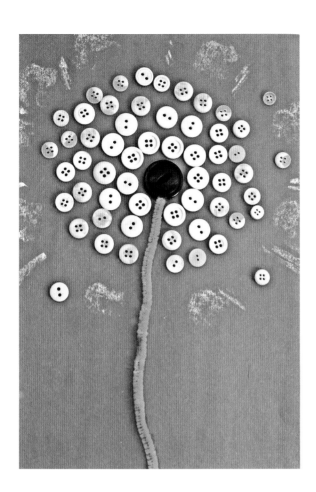

BUTTON DANDELION

To some, dandelions are considered weeds, but to children, they are just beautiful. Make a wish on your button dandelion.

SUPPLIES

- Large black button
- Construction paper
- Tacky glue
- Green pipe cleaner
- Small white buttons
- White chalk

DIRECTIONS

Glue a large black button about ⅓ of the way down from the top of a piece of construction paper. Glue a pipe cleaner directly beneath it and trim it if necessary. Glue small white buttons around the large black button spaced out slightly between each button. Use a touch of chalk to add a bit of magic around your dandelion.

BUTTON NECKLACE OR BRACELET

These are simple to make and such a fantastic fine motor activity for the kids.

SUPPLIES

- Buttons
- Pipe cleaners

DIRECTIONS

String different colored buttons on to your pipe cleaner. If you are making a bracelet, you will only need one pipe cleaner. If you will be making a necklace, you will probably need to twist a second pipe cleaner to the first. When you have strung up all the buttons that you want, twist the pipe cleaner ends together in the back.

BUTTON OCTOPUS

Octopus tentacles are fun to make. Cut out all sorts of wavy or spiral shapes.

SUPPLIES

- Purple and blue construction paper
- School glue
- Markers
- White buttons
- Googly eyes

DIRECTIONS

Cut a balloon shape out of a piece of purple construction paper to form a head. Cut eight wavy shapes out of the purple construction paper to form the arms. Position the head at the top of a piece of blue construction paper and then position the legs all around it. Glue the pieces in place. With a marker, draw lines down the center of the length of each leg. Glue the buttons to the bottom half of each leg. Glue googly eyes to the head and then draw in a mouth.

BUTTON PENGUIN

Make one or a whole bunch for a fun wintery scene with snow and ice.

SUPPLIES

- School glue
- Two large black buttons
- Blue construction paper
- Two medium black buttons
- Two small black buttons
- Two medium orange buttons
- Two large white buttons
- Googly eyes
- Orange foam

DIRECTIONS

Glue a large black button to a piece of blue construction paper for the head. To form the arms, glue the two medium black buttons diagonally to the side of the large button and then the small black buttons under the medium ones diagonally away from the body. Glue two orange buttons under the remaining large black button so that the orange peeks out at the bottom for the feet. Then glue this cluster of buttons under the head. Find two large white buttons a little smaller than the large black ones. Glue the white buttons on top of both large black buttons. Glue googly eyes to the head and then cut a small triangle out of the orange foam for the beak and then glue underneath the eyes.

BUTTON SNAKE

Stringing up buttons is great for developing fine motor skills and it is also a great screen-free distraction that will keep your children's minds and hands occupied. Make a whole family of button snakes.

SUPPLIES

- Buttons
- Pipe cleaner
- School glue
- Googly eyes
- Pink foam

DIRECTIONS

String buttons on to a pipe cleaner. Start with small buttons and work up to larger ones until you reach the middle of the pipe cleaner and then start working your way back down to smaller ones. Glue a large button to the end for the head. Add in the googly eyes and cut a small tongue out of the foam and glue onto the head.

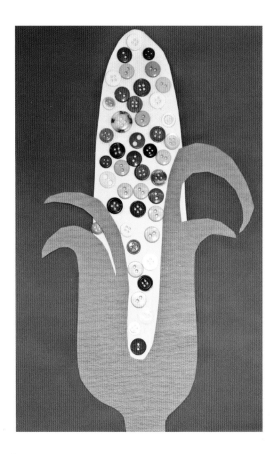

BUTTON INDIAN CORN

This would also be lovely if you mixed in corn kernels with the buttons.

SUPPLIES

- Yellow, green, and orange construction paper
- School glue
- Neutral-colored buttons

DIRECTIONS

Cut a corn cob shape out of yellow paper and a husk out of green paper. Glue the corn and the husk onto the orange paper. Glue assorted neutral colored buttons to the corn cob to form the kernels.

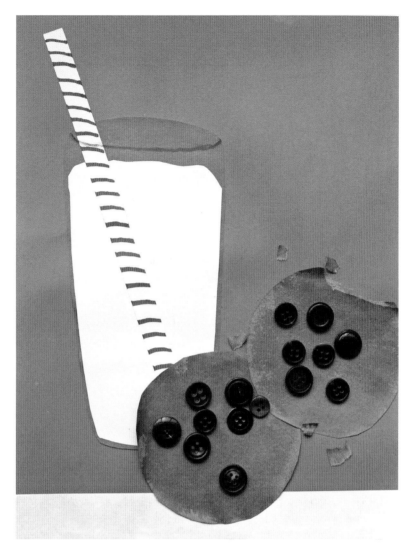

COOKIES AND MILK

You can also leave out the milk and make an assortment of paper cookies with button embellishments to play bake shop.

SUPPLIES

- Brown, blue, and white construction paper
- Brown tempura paint
- Glue stick
- Brown or black buttons
- Red marker

DIRECTIONS

Cut two circles out of brown construction paper. Paint the construction paper in brown paint to add a little texture. Let the paint dry and then glue the buttons onto the circles to form chocolate chips. Tear a few small pieces off the cookie to form crumbs. Glue your cookies to a piece of paper with the crumbs scattered all around them. Cut a glass shape out of a piece of blue construction paper and then cut a piece of white construction paper to form the white milk inside. Cut a long, narrow piece of white construction paper to form the straw and then draw curved red lines across the straw with the marker. Glue your milk next to your cookies.

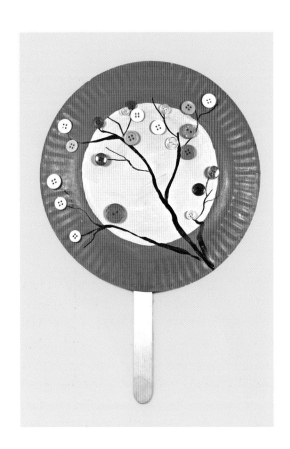

PAPER PLATE FAN

This is an easy way to make a hand fan. We used cherry blossoms, but you can use your own unique design.

SUPPLIES

- Acrylic paint
- Paper plate
- School glue
- Craft stick
- Black marker
- Pink and white buttons

DIRECTIONS

Paint the paper plate in the color of your choice and let it dry. Glue a craft stick to the bottom of the unpainted side of your paper plate for the handle. Draw branches across your paper plate with the marker. Scatter and glue buttons around the branches to form blossoms.

BUTTON RAIN

This is a great spring craft. You can even accompany this with the flower buttons for an April showers brings May flowers project.

SUPPLIES

- Construction paper
- Glue stick
- Black marker
- Blue buttons

DIRECTIONS

Cut an umbrella shape out of any color or colors of construction paper. Use a solid color or cut out different colored sections. Glue to a piece of blue construction paper. Draw in the umbrella's handle with a black marker. Glue different shades and sizes of blue buttons all around your umbrella to create button rain.

BUTTON TURTLE

Turtles are just adorable and so easy to make. Use circles to form this sweet little turtle.

SUPPLIES

- Green and blue construction paper
- Glue stick
- Green buttons
- Large googly eyes

DIRECTIONS

Cut a large circle out of a piece of green construction paper for the turtle's shell. Cut another green circle about a quarter of the size of the large one for the turtle's head. Cut four green circles roughly about half the size of the head to form the feet. Cut a small green narrow triangle for the tail. Glue the large circle to the center of the blue construction paper. Glue the head-sized circle to one side of the shell and then the triangle to the opposite end. Glue the four circles to the sides of the body, two on each end. Glue green buttons all around the shell. Glue two large googly eyes to the head.

BUTTON CATS

These button cats are adorable. Add a piece of string and make a fun bit of jewelry or an ornament.

SUPPLIES

- Large black buttons
- Glue stick
- Googly eyes
- Black foam
- Black pipe cleaners

DIRECTIONS

Overlap two large black buttons. Hold the glued buttons at a slant and then glue googly eyes inside the top button. Cut two triangles for ears out of the black foam and glue the bottom edge of the ears behind the top button. Cut a small piece of pipe cleaner and curl it slightly. Glue the pipe cleaner behind the lower button to form the tail.

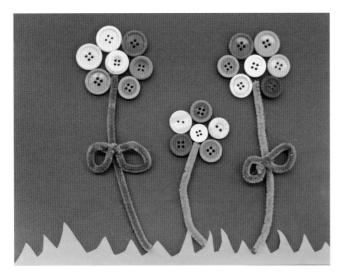

BUTTON FLOWERS

These simple button flowers are fun to make on their own or as an embellishment to another project.

SUPPLIES

- Tacky glue
- Assorted buttons
- Construction paper
- Green pipe cleaners
- Green construction paper

DIRECTIONS

Glue a yellow button to a piece of construction paper. Glue a circle of different colored buttons around it. Form more flowers around your paper following these steps, spreading them out all around your paper. Cut pieces of green pipe cleaner and glue them underneath your button clusters. Bend and curl green pipe cleaners into a bow shape to form the leaves and then glue them onto the stems. Cut jagged lines up and down on a piece of green construction paper to form grass. Glue it to the bottom of your paper.

BUTTON APPLE TREE

This adorable button tree is so sweet and simple to make. Pom-poms would also make a great option for the apples. Try making them with a thumbprint, as well.

SUPPLIES

- Green, brown, and blue construction paper
- School glue
- Red buttons

DIRECTIONS

Cut a circle out of a piece of green construction paper. Cut a simple tree trunk out of a piece of brown construction paper. Glue the trunk to a piece of blue construction paper and glue the green circle over the trunk. Glue the red buttons onto the circle to form the apples.

BUTTON ICE CREAM CONE

This cute ice cream cone would make a great wall hanging in a kid's room when finished.

SUPPLIES

- Craft sticks
- Cardboard
- School glue
- Buttons
- Brown marker

DIRECTIONS

Form a triangle with three craft sticks to form a cone. Cut a triangle out of cardboard and glue it to the back of the craft sticks. Cut a circle out of cardboard and glue it to the back of your cone. Pick buttons in the color or colors that you want your ice cream to be and glue them to the front of the circle. Glue the larger buttons down first and then add in the smaller ones to fill in the blank spaces. Overlap some of the buttons over the top of the cone. Draw crisscrosses with brown marker across the cardboard inside of the cone to finish it off.

CHAPTER THREE

CLAY CREATIONS

Whichever clay you choose to use, clay is a wonderful outlet for your child's creativity. Just molding and feeling the clay also offers a wonderful sensory experience for your children.

Craft #1: Clay & Pipe Cleaner Dinosaur

Craft #2: Clay Beads

Craft #3: Clay Fossils

Craft #4: Clay Key Chains

Craft #5: Clay Lollipop

Craft #6: Clay Magnets

Craft #7: Clay Monsters

Craft #8: Clay Nature Island

Craft #9: Clay Tribal Mask

Craft #10: Clay Volcano

Craft #11: Clay-Wrapped Branch

Craft #12: Pinch Pots

Craft #13: Polymer Clay Rainbow

Craft #14: Clay Thumbprint Heart

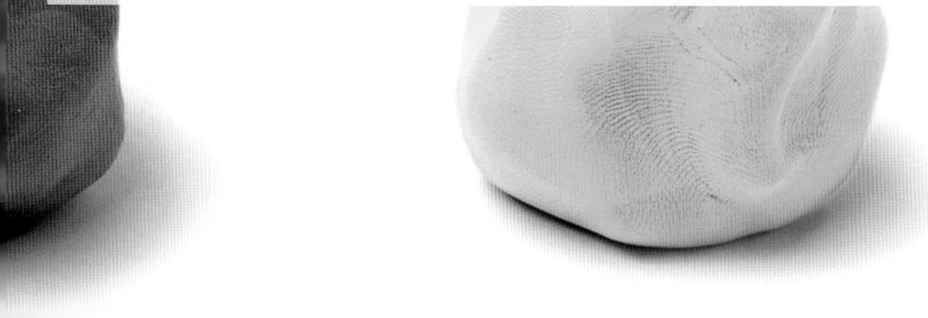

CLAY & PIPE CLEANER DINOSAUR

SUPPLIES

- Air dry clay
- Pipe cleaners
- Acrylic paint
- Tacky glue
- Googly eyes

DIRECTIONS

Form a dinosaur's body by shaping the clay. Mold legs and a tail. Cut a few pipe cleaners in half and curve them. Stick them into the clay to form spikes. Let the clay dry for a day or two and then paint the body in the color or colors of your choice. Glue the googly eyes into place when the paint dries.

CLAY BEADS

Polymer clay is wonderful for making jewelry. You can use your beads to make a necklace, bracelet, or even earrings. Try rolling out strands to form bangles or twist different shapes to make pendants.

SUPPLIES

- Polymer clay
- Butter knife
- Wooden skewer
- Necklace string
- Necklace clasp

DIRECTIONS

Pick a few different colors of clay for your beads. Grab a chunk of polymer clay from each color and roll together to marble the colors. Roll your clay into a long strip about a ½ inch thick. Use the knife to cut ½-inch sections. Roll each section into a ball. With a skewer, poke the balls through the center to form a hole in each. Bake the clay according to the package directions and then let them cool. String the beads onto a necklace string and tie the ends to a clasp.

CLAY FOSSILS

You can take this a step further and add the fossils to a sensory bin covered with sand for a fun archeologist's dig.

SUPPLIES

- Air dry clay
- Toy dinosaurs
- Acrylic paint

DIRECTIONS

Roll a ball of clay between your palms. Flatten your ball with your hands and form a flat shape or use a cookie cutter. Press a dinosaur toy into the clay and set it aside to let the clay dry. When the clay has dried, paint the clay in soft earth-toned colors.

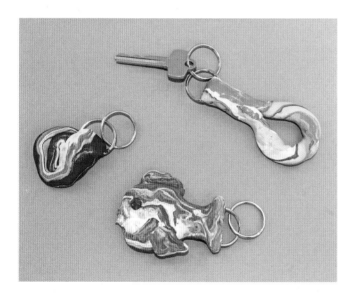

CLAY KEY CHAINS

Key chains are fun, easy to make, and are a great kid-made gift.

SUPPLIES

- Polymer clay
- Key chain rings

DIRECTIONS

Form a shape or an object with your clay. Wrap your clay around one end of a key chain ring to mold it onto the ring. Bake your clay with the ring on it per the clay's package directions. Be careful removing the key chains from the oven as the clay and especially the rings will be hot. Use for your own keys or give as a gift. Adult assistance is recommended when using the oven.

CLAY LOLLIPOP

Make an assortment of lollipops. You can also form wonderful wrapped candies, such as peppermints. Some of the candies or lollipops can appear lifelike, so be sure to keep out of reach of small children as they may mistake them for real candy.

SUPPLIES

- Air dry clay
- Cake pop stick
- Acrylic paint

DIRECTIONS

Roll out a long, thin strand of clay. Start in the middle and coil your strand into a circle. Press the stick into the back of your lollipop and then let the clay dry. For added support for your stick, add a little extra clay over the stick to hold it into place. Once your clay has dried, use different colored paints and paint swirls around your lollipop.

CLAY MAGNETS

Magnets are so easy to make, and there are so many possibilities with these clay magnets. These would make a great gift idea, too.

SUPPLIES

- Air dry clay
- Rolling pin
- Cookie cutters
- Magnet strips
- Acrylic paint

DIRECTIONS

Roll a ball of air dry clay between your palms. Roll out the clay with a rolling pin. Use a cookie cutter on your clay or free form your own shape. Cut a piece of magnet from a magnet roll or use precut magnet strips. Press the magnet onto the back end of your clay and set it aside to dry. This may take a day or two. Paint a picture or design onto your clay once it has dried. If the magnet wiggles free, use glue to secure it.

CLAY MONSTERS

Monsters are so much fun to make because there are really no rules—you can make them in any shape or size. Polymer clay is great to use for this. You can use a large variety of colors and the polymer clay molds very well. The best thing about polymer clay is, unless you bake it, it stays soft and moldable and can be used again and again.

SUPPLIES

- Rolling pin
- Polymer clay
- Googly eyes
- Buttons

DIRECTIONS

Roll the clay out into any kind of shape. Add as many googly eyes as you like. Make teeth or horns out of the clay. Use buttons to form a mouth. Use pipe cleaners to form arms or legs if you choose. If you're going to bake the clay, do not bake the polymer monsters with the googly eyes and the other accessories already attached—the plastic will warp in the oven.

CLAY NATURE ISLAND

Half the fun of this project is searching for the supplies outside.

SUPPLIES

- Acrylic paint
- Paper plate
- Air dry clay
- Twig, pebbles, leaves, flowers

DIRECTIONS

Paint a paper plate blue to look like water. Set the plate aside to let it dry. Form a large mound of clay and press it into the center of the paper plate. Collect leaves, pebbles, and small flowers from the outdoors and then press them into the clay so that flowers and plants stick up straight. Keep adding nature items to form your island.

CLAY TRIBAL MASK

You can make small mini masks, as well.

SUPPLIES

- Air dry clay
- Rolling pin
- Paper plate
- Toothpick
- Acrylic paint
- School glue
- Gemstones

DIRECTIONS

Grab a large handful of air dry clay and roll out a circle the size of a paper plate. Mold a nose shape and blend it into the center of the circle. Lay your clay over a paper plate and allow it to curve around. Use your fingers to press indentations into the clay for the eyes and a mouth. Dampen the clay slightly to fix any imperfections. Let the clay dry for a day or two. Use a toothpick to carve in lines and designs. Clean up any crumbs. Paint your masks in the colors of your choice. Glue gemstones to the eyes, mouth, and cheeks. Remove the paper plate.

CLAY VOLCANO

Make mini clay volcanos out of the paper cups and form a clay island around them.

SUPPLIES

- Paper cup
- Paper bowl
- Air dry clay
- Acrylic paint

DIRECTIONS

Cut the bottom of a paper cup off. Place the paper cup bottom-side up on top of the bowl. Grab some clay and start molding around the cup and bowl. Keep molding until you form your volcano. Let your volcano dry for a day or two. Paint your volcano in brown acrylic paint, squeeze red acrylic paint along the top, and then set it aside to let it dry.

CLAY-WRAPPED BRANCH

Another alternative to a fully covered branch is to use blobs of clay to press into the smaller branches to make a tree-like craft using the clay as leaves.

SUPPLIES

- Polymer clay
- Branch or a stick

DIRECTIONS

Break off chunks of different colored polymer clay and press and form the clay around a branch or a stick.

PINCH POTS

Pinch pots are easy and fun to make and are very useful when finished. Make a collection of them to hold and organize various items.

SUPPLIES

- Air dry clay
- Acrylic paint

DIRECTIONS

Roll out a ball of clay between your palms. The size of your ball will depend on how large you would like your pinch pot to be. Begin pressing into the top of your ball with your thumbs to form your bowl. Hollow out your bowl by pressing in with your thumbs and pinching along the outside edge of the clay. Let the clay pots dry. It may take a day or two to dry fully. Once they are dry, paint the pinch pots in the color or colors of your choice.

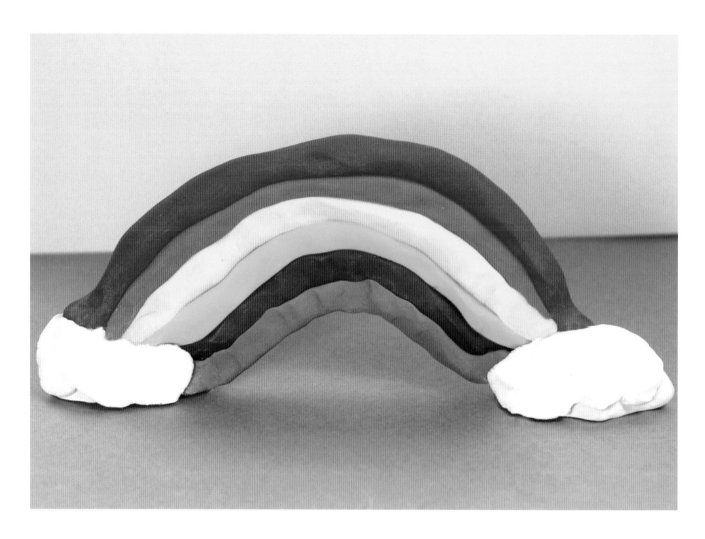

POLYMER CLAY RAINBOW

Polymer clay is wonderful to work with; it does not crumble or dry up until you bake it. It's easy and smooth to work with and the colors blend beautifully.

SUPPLIES
- Polymer clay (rainbow colors)
- White polymer clay

DIRECTIONS

Roll out each rainbow color between your palms to form a long strand. Curve and lay the red strand down and then curve the orange strand right beneath it, then add the yellow, green, blue, and purple. Gently press each color into the next as you arrange them. Form two white masses for clouds, and press either end of the rainbow into each cloud. Bake your project according to the clay's package directions to harden.

CLAY THUMBPRINT HEART

Make your thumbprint into a key chain or an ornament or curl the sides up a bit to form a small dish. Whatever you choose to make, it will make a lovely keepsake.

SUPPLIES

- Air dry clay
- Rolling pin
- Circle cookie cutter
- Straw
- Acrylic paint
- Ribbon

DIRECTIONS

Grab a clump of air dry clay. Use a rolling pin to roll out the clay. Use a cookie cutter to cut out a circle. Press a thumb at a slant in the center of the clay. Press a thumb slanted in the opposite direction to form a heart shape. Use a straw to poke a hole through the top of the circle. Let the clay dry for one to two days and then paint the inside of the heart. Let the paint dry and then cut a piece of ribbon or string and thread it through the hole to hang.

CHAPTER FOUR

CONSTRUCTION PAPER CRAFTS

You can make just about anything with construction paper. Just cut a bunch of simple shapes and see what you can dream up.

Craft #1: 3-D Clown Fish

Craft #2: Build a Barn

Craft #3: Cut & Curl Sheep

Craft #4: Happy Face Clock

Craft #5: Mosaic Watermelon

Craft #6: Paper Lei

Craft #7: Paper City

Craft #8: Emotion Masks

Craft #9: Pirate Eye Patch

Craft #10: Pretty Pansy

Craft #11: Shape Giraffe

Craft #12: Shape Poodle

Craft #13: Shape Rocket

Craft #14: Stuffed Football

Craft #15: Wizard's Hat

3-D CLOWN FISH

Smaller children may prefer this as a two-dimensional craft. The three-dimensional fish offers a fine motor component for those looking for something a little more advanced.

SUPPLIES

- Orange, white, and blue construction paper
- Glue stick
- Large googly eye

DIRECTIONS

Cut strips of white and orange construction paper in ascending and descending sizes. Cut a fish head and tail out of the orange construction paper. Glue the head to a piece of blue construction paper. Line up the strips in alternating colors going from small to large and then back down to small again. Apply glue just to the ends of each of the strips and glue them next to the head. Glue down just the ends and let the center of each strip form an arc protruding off of the paper. Glue the tail into place and then add a googly eye to the head to finish off your fish.

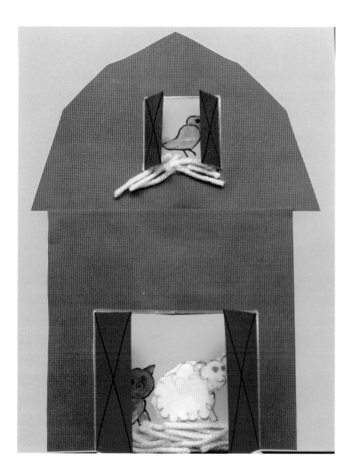

BUILD A BARN

You could use this peekaboo idea with a number of different structures. Open doors and windows to a house or school and draw what is inside.

SUPPLIES

- Red and blue construction paper
- Glue stick
- Yellow yarn
- Markers, acrylic paint, or crayons

DIRECTIONS

Cut a large square shape out of a piece of red construction paper. Cut up from the bottom center of the square about halfway up and then cut to the left and then to the right, just enough to form a foldable flap on each side to form the barn doors. Cut a roof shape out of a piece of red construction paper and then cut door flaps into the center of the roof. You will have to poke a small hole into the center to start your first cut. Use caution when poking your hole. Glue both barn pieces to a piece of blue construction paper, but keep the doors open so that you do not glue them down. Cut small strands of yarn to form straw and hay and then glue them to the inside of your doors along the bottom edge of your door openings. Use markers, paint, or crayons to draw animals inside your barn.

CUT & CURL SHEEP

This is a great activity to practice scissor skills.

SUPPLIES

- White and blue construction paper
- School glue
- Cotton balls
- Large googly eyes
- Markers

DIRECTIONS

Cut two circles out of a piece of white construction paper. Place one of the circles onto the bottom half of a piece of blue construction paper. Glue just the upper third of the circle down to the paper. Overlap the second cut circle over the first circle about an inch higher and only glue the top third again. You want the bottom of both circles to be loose and unattached. Cut long, narrow strips starting from the bottom of each circle about halfway up. Use a pencil to curl each strip upward and toward the body. Glue the legs into place after curling all of the strips. Cut an oval shape for the head and glue it to the upper portion of the top circle. Cut ears and legs out of the white construction paper and then glue both into place. Stretch and glue the cotton balls onto the top of the head. Glue on the googly eyes and then draw in the nose and mouth with markers.

HAPPY FACE CLOCK

These have movable hands perfect for learning how to tell time.

SUPPLIES

- Construction paper (any color)
- Tacky glue
- Number stickers
- Split pin
- Large googly eyes
- Marker

DIRECTIONS

Cut a large circle out of a piece of construction paper. Cut another circle a bit smaller than the first in a different colored piece of construction paper. Glue the smaller circle onto the larger one. Place your number stickers around the outer edge of the inner circle. Cut your big hand and little hand out of a different colored construction paper and poke a split pin through each hand and then through the center of the clock. Glue the googly eyes onto the top of the clock and then use a marker to draw in the smile.

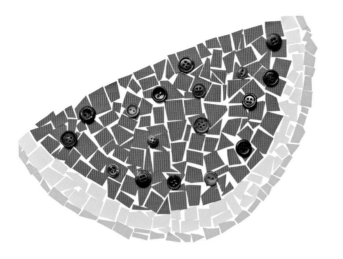

MOSAIC WATERMELON

Mosaics are pretty and fun to make. You can use a variety of different materials to form mosaics. You can use paper, tissue, rocks, or pasta.

SUPPLIES

- Red, green, white, and light green construction paper
- Glue stick
- Black buttons

DIRECTIONS

Cut the red, green, and light green construction papers into small pieces. Draw a very faint picture of a watermelon on a piece of white construction paper. Fill in your sketch by gluing the small pieces inside your sketch. Be sure to leave space between pieces as often as you can, but it is fine if the pieces overlap a bit. Glue the red pieces into the main fleshy area, the light green pieces underneath for the inner rind, and then the darker green pieces for the outside rind. After you fill in your sketch with the pieces, glue black buttons over the red paper to represent the seeds.

PAPER LEI

Aloha! You don't need to go to a luau to make these pretty and colorful leis. Leis are fun for all ages.

SUPPLIES

- Construction paper
- Yarn needle
- Yarn

DIRECTIONS

Cut a simple flower shape out of a piece of construction paper. Use that shape as a template and then cut out many more in assorted colors. You can cut out a few at a time to make it quicker. We used close to forty shapes. Thread the yarn needle with yarn. Poke the yarn needle through the center of your flowers. Continue to string your flowers until your lei has reached the desired length and tie a knot on the end.

PAPER CITY

You could stand up your paper city for a great backdrop in pretend play. I bet the egg carton cars from the Recyclables with a Purpose chapter would love to go for a drive in the city at night.

SUPPLIES

- Acrylic paint
- Watercolor paper
- Black construction paper
- Glue stick
- Cotton swab

DIRECTIONS

Paint a night sky on a piece of watercolor paper using black, purple, gray, or pink acrylic paint. Let the paint dry. Cut different sized rectangles out of a piece or two of black construction paper. Cut some taller and some shorter. Glue the different shapes to the night sky. Layer the shapes with the taller shapes in the back. Use your finger or a cotton swab to dab on white and yellow paints to form the window lights. Cut out peaks and smoke stacks to add to the tops of your buildings.

EMOTION MASKS

Children have many different emotions that they don't always understand. These are fun to make and a wonderful tool for teaching your children about all of those different feelings. Make happy faces, sad, silly, and scared or any other emotions that you can come up with.

SUPPLIES

- Construction paper
- School glue
- Large googly eyes
- Markers
- Craft sticks

DIRECTIONS

Cut different colored construction papers into large face-sized circles. Glue googly eyes onto each circle. Draw a smiley face or a frown for a happy or sad face. Make a zigzag mouth for an angry face, an "O" mouth for a surprised face, or stick out a tongue if you are feeling a bit silly. Glue a craft stick to the back of each of your circles to make a handle for your masks.

PIRATE EYE PATCH

Arg, me mateys! This is a quick little craft that would be perfect for your little pirates. Pair this up with the telescope from the Recyclables with a Purpose chapter and the treasure map from the Tissue Paper chapter and you have a great opportunity for some pretend pirate fun.

SUPPLIES

- Black foam
- Black construction paper
- Black yarn
- Tacky glue
- White paint

DIRECTIONS

Cut the shape of your eye patch out of a piece of black foam and then cut a smaller version of that shape out of black construction paper. Measure out and cut a piece of yarn big enough to fit around your head. Glue each end of the yarn to each side of the foam. Glue the construction paper over the yarn and foam. Paint a skull and crossbones on the paper and then let it dry.

PRETTY PANSY

Many crafts and drawings can be formed by using simple shapes. Create a whole garden of flowers using different shapes. Make petals out of diamonds, circles, or even rectangles.

SUPPLIES

- Construction paper (any color)
- Glue stick

DIRECTIONS

Cut four petal shapes out of construction paper in the color of your choice. Choose a different color and then cut three heart shapes a bit smaller than the petals. The hearts should be able to fit into the petals. Cut a circle out of a different color and then cut a stem and leaf out of green construction paper. Glue the three hearts into three of the petals. Glue the plain petal to the top of a piece of construction paper. Glue and overlap two of the heart-filled petals onto the side of the plain petal. Glue the last heart-filled petal to the point where the two side petals meet. Glue the circle to the center of your flower and then glue on the stem and the leaf.

SHAPE GIRAFFE

If you have a child that doesn't like to dip their hands in paint, use buttons or tear up pieces of brown paper to form the giraffe's spots.

SUPPLIES

- Yellow and blue construction paper
- Glue stick
- Cotton swab
- Brown tempura paint
- Googly eye
- Marker

DIRECTIONS

For your giraffe, you will need to cut a number of shapes out of yellow construction paper. Cut out a large rectangle for the body, a long narrow rectangle for the neck, and an oval for the head. You will also need four narrow rectangles for the legs, one narrow rectangle for the tail, and then two ovals for the ears and two small rectangles for the ossicones (giraffe horns). Put your shapes together to form the giraffe and glue to a piece of blue construction paper. Dip a finger or use a cotton swab to dab the spots onto the giraffe with brown paint. Glue the googly eye in place. Use a marker to draw in a nose and mouth.

SHAPE POODLE

A paper bowl can also be used for the main part of the body to add a little dimension to your craft.

SUPPLIES

- White construction paper
- School glue
- Black button
- Googly eye
- White pom-poms or cotton balls

DIRECTIONS

Cut a circle, an oval, and five narrow rectangles out of a piece of white construction paper. Glue the circle to the center of a piece of paper. Glue the oval shape to the upper side of the circle at a slant. This will be the head. Glue one of the rectangles to the center of the opposite side of the circle to form the tail. Glue the remaining four rectangles to the bottom of the circle to form the legs. Glue a button to the lower end of the oval for the nose. Glue on a googly eye. Add your pom-poms or cotton balls to the end of the tail and legs and then to the top of the head and the body.

SHAPE ROCKET

3, 2, 1—blast off to outer space. Rocket ships and space are a favorite of boys and girls.

SUPPLIES

- Construction paper (any colors)
- Glue stick
- Red tissue paper
- Silver marker

DIRECTIONS

Gather different colored construction paper. Cut three triangles, a square, a long rectangle, and a circle out of the different colored construction papers. Glue the shapes onto a piece of black construction paper. Glue the triangle to the top of the black paper with the square beneath it. Glue the rectangle underneath it and then the other two triangles to the side of the rectangle. Glue the circle into the center of the square. Cut strips out of the red tissue paper and twist to form rocket fire. Glue to the bottom of the rectangle. Draw stars and planets around your rocket with a silver marker to finish it off.

STUFFED FOOTBALL

This is great for your little sports fans.

SUPPLIES

- Light brown and white construction paper
- Dark brown acrylic paint
- Tacky glue
- Tissue paper

DIRECTIONS

Cut two football shapes out of a piece of brown construction paper. Paint over them with brown paint and let the two pieces dry. Cut shapes out of the white construction paper to form the lacing. Glue the lacing to both sides. Glue or staple the two bottom halves of your footballs together. Lightly stuff the inside of your football with the tissue paper and then seal the remainder of the football.

WIZARD'S HAT

This same concept can also be used during Halloween to make a witch's hat.

SUPPLIES

- Acrylic paint
- 12 x 12 card stock
- Paper plate
- Tape
- Tacky glue
- Black and silver markers
- Optional: glitter, stickers

DIRECTIONS

Choose the color that you would like for your hat. Find a paint and a piece of card stock close in color to use together. Cut the center of a paper plate out and paint it in that color. Cut two pieces of card stock in the color of your choice in the shape shown in Fig. 1. Curve both pieces of card stock toward each other and have them hug each other to form a cone. Leave a small opening at the top of your cone. When you get your cone to the width that you want, tape the cone into place. Glue the cone into the hole in the paper plate. Roll a skinny cone out of another piece of card stock and stick it up through the top of the opening and then bend it to the side to form the hat's tip. Use markers, stickers, glitter, and any other embellishments to decorate your hat.

Fig. 1

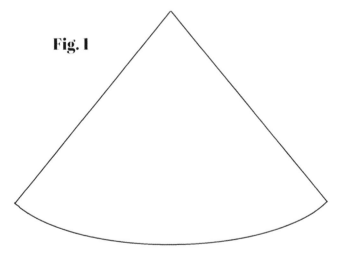

CHAPTER FIVE

CRAFT STICK CRAFTS

I love craft sticks. You can build with them, craft with them—you can even paint with them. They are a must for every craft room.

Craft #1: Craft Stick Bookmark

Craft #2: Craft Stick Butterfly

Craft #3: Craft Stick Captain's Wheel

Craft #4: Craft Stick Crayons

Craft #5: Craft Stick Fire Truck

Craft #6: Craft Stick Horse

Craft #7: Craft Stick Kite

Craft #8: Craft Stick Owl

Craft #9: Craft Stick Peacock

Craft #10: Craft Stick Puzzle

Craft #11: Craft Stick Robot

Craft #12: Craft Stick Sailboat

Craft #13: Craft Stick Windmill

Craft #14: Nature Fence

Craft #15: Craft Stick Window Suncatcher

Craft #16: Craft Stick Xylophone

Craft #17: Craft Stick Twinkle Star

Craft #18: Magnet Frame

CRAFT STICK BOOKMARK

Bookmarks always come in handy. Make bookmarks with different inspirational sayings or designs on them.

SUPPLIES

- Tacky glue
- Jumbo craft sticks
- Acrylic paint
- Marker
- Yarn

DIRECTIONS

Glue two craft sticks next to each other vertically. Paint the craft sticks in the color and design of your choosing and let them dry. For ours, we simply spelled out the word "read." Use a marker to outline your design to help make it stand out. Braid yarn together and tie off on both ends. Glue one end to the top of the craft sticks to finish off your bookmark.

CRAFT STICK BUTTERFLY

Butterflies are beautiful and fun to design. You are not limited to just using buttons. Add glitter, sequins, stickers, or any embellishments of your choosing to create your pretty butterfly.

SUPPLIES

- Acrylic paint
- Jumbo craft stick
- Construction paper or foam sheets
- Tacky glue
- Markers
- Buttons
- Googly eyes
- Pipe cleaners

DIRECTIONS

Paint the craft stick in the color of your choosing and let it dry. Cut four heart shapes in any color out of a piece of construction paper or foam. Glue the shapes to the back of the craft stick to form wings. Decorate the wings with markers and buttons. Glue googly eyes onto the stick and then glue pipe cleaners on for the antennae.

CRAFT STICK CAPTAIN'S WHEEL

SUPPLIES

- Acrylic paint
- Paper plate
- Jumbo craft sticks
- Tacky glue
- Buttons
- Yarn

DIRECTIONS

Paint a paper plate in the color of your choice and then let the paint dry. Cut out the center of the paper plate at the first crease in the plate. Cut a circle about 4 inches round out of the piece that you just cut out. Glue eight craft sticks around the unpainted side of the 4-inch inner circle cutout. Space them out an equal distance. Glue the outer ring of the paper plate onto the craft sticks, keeping the circle cutout in the center. Glue buttons to the outer edge of the craft sticks and then wrap yarn around the outer paper plate ring to finish it off.

CRAFT STICK CRAYONS

You can use this same concept to make pencils for a great back to school craft idea.

SUPPLIES

- Acrylic paint
- Jumbo craft sticks
- Colored foam sheets
- Tacky glue
- Markers
- Construction paper (any color)

DIRECTIONS

Paint a craft stick in each color of the spectrum and then set them all aside to dry. Cut a small triangular piece and a small rectangular piece of each color of the spectrum out of the foam sheets. Glue the triangular piece to the top of the coordinating craft stick for the crayon tip and then glue the rectangular piece to the bottom for the bottom of the crayon. Use a marker to draw lines and squiggles to add details to the crayons. Fold a piece of construction paper around the crayons to form a crayon box.

CRAFT STICK FIRE TRUCK

This would be a great craft to make while discussing fire safety. Use tissue paper or paint a fire in the background to expand on your project.

SUPPLIES

- Acrylic paint
- Jumbo craft sticks
- Tacky glue
- Large black buttons
- Red and white foam sheets
- Marker

DIRECTIONS

Paint eight craft sticks in red paint and let them dry. Cut three of the sticks in half. Glue the four uncut sticks together side by side so that the sticks are horizontal. Glue five of the stick halves together side by side the same way. Place the half sticks to the left of the whole ones. Snip about one-third off of the remaining craft stick and then overlap and glue it so that it joins the two sections together. Glue three large buttons to the bottom as wheels. Cut a small square out of a piece of white foam to form a window and then glue it into place. Cut a small rounded red shape for the siren and glue it to the top. With a black marker, draw a ladder onto an unpainted craft stick and then glue it on as shown.

CRAFT STICK HORSE

Clothespins and crafts sticks are a great combination. Play around and discover other fun crafts or clip the clothespins to craft sticks for a unique engineering opportunity or to make wooden sculptures.

SUPPLIES

- Brown acrylic paint
- Craft stick
- Four clothespins
- Brown foam
- Brown yarn
- Tacky glue
- Googly eyes
- Mini cupcake liner

DIRECTIONS

Paint the craft stick and clothespins brown and set them aside to dry. Cut a horse head shape out of a piece of brown foam. Cut strands of brown yarn and glue them to the top of the horse's head for the mane. Glue the googly eyes to the head. Clip the four clothespins onto the craft stick into two upside down "V" shapes. Clip the horse's head onto one of the clothespins on the end. Glue strands of yarn to the opposite end of the head to form the tail. Fold and glue a mini cupcake liner around the middle of the craft stick for the saddle.

CRAFT STICK KITE

Try this with wax paper layered with craft tissue in lieu of the painted paper for a great suncatcher to hang in your window.

SUPPLIES

- Black acrylic paint
- Jumbo craft sticks
- Tacky glue
- Watercolor paper
- Watercolor paint
- Pipe cleaner

DIRECTIONS

Paint six craft sticks in black acrylic paint and let the sticks dry. Glue four craft sticks together to form a diamond shape. Form a cross with the other two craft sticks and then glue it to the middle of the diamond. Cut a diamond shape in the same size as the kite out of a piece of watercolor paper. Cut three bow shapes out of watercolor paper and use watercolors to paint all of the shapes. Set them aside to dry. Glue the triangle-shaped paper behind your kite shape. Glue a pipe cleaner to your triangle for your kite string and then glue the painted bows onto the pipe cleaner.

CRAFT STICK OWL

When painting your owl, don't be afraid to play with color. Make a pink owl or a speckled owl or just a mash-up of all kinds of colors.

SUPPLIES

- Tacky glue
- Jumbo craft sticks
- Acrylic paint
- Foam sheets
- Large googly eyes
- Feathers

DIRECTIONS

Glue four craft sticks together side by side vertically. Paint your craft sticks in the color of your choice. This will be the owl's body. Cut two large circles out of a piece of foam for the eyes. Cut two smaller circles out of a different colored piece of foam and then glue the smaller circles inside the larger circles. Glue the googly eyes inside the center of the smaller circles to finish your eyes. Glue the eyes to the top of the craft sticks. Cut a small triangle out of orange foam for the beak and then glue it into place. Glue feathers to the sides for the wings.

CRAFT STICK PEACOCK

Don't feel limited to buttons for decorating your peacocks. Try adding sequins, feathers, pieces of paper, or tissue, or use swirls of paint to paint on the peacock feather designs.

SUPPLIES

- Acrylic paint
- 12 jumbo craft sticks
- Tacky glue
- Googly eyes
- Orange construction paper
- Buttons

DIRECTIONS

Paint two craft sticks in blue and then paint ten more in a shade of green. Let the paint dry. Glue the two blue craft sticks together side by side vertically and then fan out the ten green sticks and glue them to the unpainted side of the two blue sticks. Let the glue dry and then glue a pair of googly eyes and an orange beak onto the front of the blue craft sticks. Glue different shades of blue, green, and white buttons to the fanned-out craft sticks to decorate.

CRAFT STICK PUZZLE

You can make these as small or large as you like. These are a great beginner puzzle, too, for smaller children. Make a bunch of puzzles and keep them separated with rubber bands.

SUPPLIES

- Jumbo craft sticks
- Tape
- Acrylic paint or markers

DIRECTIONS

Line up six or more craft sticks side by side vertically or diagonally. Use a piece or two of tape to hold the sticks together on one side. Flip the sticks over and use markers or paint to make a picture. Let it dry if needed. Remove the tape and mix up the sticks and then put the pieces back together as a puzzle.

CRAFT STICK ROBOT

Robots are great fun to make. This is just one suggestion, but there are a ton of possibilities when making a robot. Challenge your kid to make them using paper shapes, recycled cans, or toilet paper tubes. Try clay with pasta arms and legs. Anything goes.

SUPPLIES

- Acrylic paint
- Jumbo craft sticks
- Tacky glue
- Black foam
- Pipe cleaners
- Googly eyes
- Buttons

DIRECTIONS

Paint five craft sticks in silver acrylic paint and then set them aside to dry. Glue four of the sticks side by side vertically and then glue the fifth stick in the middle of these with about two inches sticking up over the top of it. Cut a rectangle out of foam and glue it to the protruding stick. Twist and glue pipe cleaners to the back of the craft sticks to form arms and legs. Glue googly eyes to the foam piece and add buttons as embellishments.

CRAFT STICK SAILBOAT

Paint an ocean backdrop for your sailboat and glue your finished sailboat onto it for a wonderful nautical scene.

SUPPLIES

- Acrylic paint
- Jumbo craft sticks
- Tacky glue
- White and blue foam

DIRECTIONS

Paint three craft sticks in the color of your choice and then paint one more in a different color. Let the sticks dry. Glue the three same-colored sticks together horizontally. Glue the other stick vertically to one of the sides. Cut a piece of white foam into a triangle and glue to the vertical stick for the sail. Cut out a simple wave design and glue it to the bottom of your boat to finish it off.

CRAFT STICK WINDMILL

To make a windmill with spinning blades, just trade the craft stick blades out for cardstock and insert a split pin into the peak of the construction paper.

SUPPLIES

- Tacky glue
- Jumbo craft sticks
- Acrylic paint
- Large button
- Construction paper or foam sheets
- Markers

DIRECTIONS

Glue three craft sticks together to form a triangle. Paint the triangle in the color of your choice and then set it aside to let it dry. Glue four sticks together to form an "X" shape and then paint the shape and set it aside to dry. Glue the X to the top point of the triangle and glue a large button to the center of the X to form the blades. Cut a triangle out of a piece of construction paper or foam. (I prefer foam for durability.) Glue the triangle to the unpainted side of the craft stick triangle. Use a marker to draw in a door and windows for your windmill.

NATURE FENCE

You can opt to pick your own flowers outside or use foam flowers or stickers to decorate your fences. You can always mix it up and combine both natural and foam flowers and leaves.

SUPPLIES

- Jumbo craft sticks
- Tacky glue
- Acrylic paint
- Real or foam flowers

DIRECTIONS

Lay three craft sticks down vertically. Space them out a bit. Overlap and glue two sets of craft sticks together to form a line. Glue one of the lines on the top about a ¼ of an inch down from the top and then the other to the bottom about ¼ of an inch up. Let your glue dry and paint your fence. Pick and glue real flowers to your fence or use foam flowers to decorate your fence.

CRAFT STICK WINDOW SUNCATCHER

A great activity for every season! Have the child or children look outside and draw what they see. This can also be done as a simple stained glass window by drawing in shapes or squiggles and then painting.

SUPPLIES

- Jumbo craft sticks
- Tacky glue
- Wax paper
- Black Sharpie
- Acrylic paint
- Tape
- String

DIRECTIONS

To form a window with your craft stick, first glue four craft sticks together to form a square and then glue one stick across the center vertically and then another across the center horizontally. Cut a piece of wax paper big enough to fit behind the window. Use a Sharpie to draw an outdoor scene or just an abstract design onto the wax paper. Let the Sharpie dry and then flip the wax paper over. Paint the pattern or picture on the backside of the wax paper. After the paint dries, tape the wax paper onto the frame with the Sharpie side peeking out of the window. Hang your window with double-sided tape or string.

CRAFT STICK XYLOPHONE

This craft could also be a great opportunity to learn about color blending. Paint a stick in red and yellow to form the orange; blue and yellow to form the green; and red and blue to form the purple.

SUPPLIES
- Acrylic paint
- Jumbo craft sticks
- Tacky glue

DIRECTIONS

Paint six craft sticks in each of the colors of the rainbow. Let the sticks dry. Place two unpainted sticks in a line at a slant. Line up two more sticks next to the first set. Slant them in the other direction so that the sticks form an open "V" shape for the body of the xylophone. Start from the wide end and glue the red craft stick across the top of the body. Leave some space and glue the orange below the red stick. Glue the yellow stick below the orange at the area where the two unpainted sticks meet so that it connects the sticks. Continue gluing the rest of the craft sticks down the line in the order of which they fall in the color spectrum.

CRAFT STICK TWINKLE STAR

Star crafts fit with a variety of themes. Stars can be related to outer space, Christmas, Fourth of July, or something more magical.

SUPPLIES
- Tacky glue
- Craft sticks
- Acrylic paint
- Glitter
- Pipe cleaner or yarn

DIRECTIONS

Glue the craft sticks together to form a star. Paint the star in the color of your choice. Sprinkle glitter over the wet paint and let the paint dry. Use a pipe cleaner or yarn to hang.

MAGNET FRAME

If your children like to display their artwork on the refrigerator, this would be a great idea to have them showcase some of their favorite artwork. Make a larger frame by adding additional craft sticks. This would also make a wonderful homemade gift for a lucky family member.

SUPPLIES

- Tacky glue
- Jumbo craft sticks
- Acrylic paint
- Buttons
- Magnet pieces

DIRECTIONS

Glue two craft sticks together side by side. Repeat this step three more times and then glue the four sections together to form a square frame. Let the glue dry. Paint the craft sticks with any color acrylic paint and then let them dry. Add buttons or any embellishments of your choice. Glue magnet pieces to the back of the frame and then tape your favorite family photo or drawing to the back.

CHAPTER SIX

CUPCAKE LINER CRAFTS

Cupcake liners are not just for baking delicious treats; they also make delightful crafts!

Craft #1: Cupcake Liner Balloons

Craft #2: Cupcake Liner Banjo

Craft #3: Cupcake Liner Baseball

Craft #4: Cupcake Liner Bumblebee

Craft #5: Cupcake Liner Clown

Craft #6: Cupcake Liner Lizard

Craft #7: Cupcake Liner Pig

Craft #8: Cupcake Liner Pup

Craft #9: Cupcake Liner Scarecrow

Craft #10: Cupcake Liner Seashells

Craft #11: Cupcake Liner Submarine

Craft #12: Cupcake Liner Sunflower

Craft #13: Cupcake Liner Tractor

Craft #14: Cupcake Liner Lily Pads

CUPCAKE LINER BALLOONS

You may also glue the balloons flat to the paper. Try mini cupcake liners to add even more balloons.

SUPPLIES

- Glue stick
- Cupcake liners
- Blue construction paper
- Markers
- White yarn
- Cotton balls
- School glue

DIRECTIONS

Use a glue stick to glue the outer edge of each cupcake liner. Press just the outer edge of the liners onto a piece of blue construction paper so that the center puffs out. Select markers in the same color as the cupcake liners and draw the lips of the balloons under each liner. Cut long pieces of yarn to form the balloon strings and then glue them beneath the balloons. Stretch out cotton balls and glue around the balloons to form clouds.

CUPCAKE LINER BANJO

With some assistance from an adult, you can use a rubber band in place of the yarn. Cut the rubber band in half and then lengthwise. Staple it to the banjo and strum the bands.

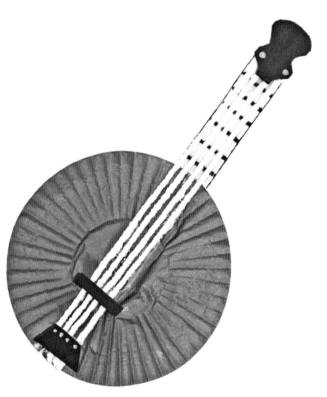

SUPPLIES

- Tacky glue
- Craft stick
- Cupcake liner (any color)
- Black and silver marker
- Yarn
- Black construction paper

DIRECTIONS

Glue a craft stick to the back of a cupcake liner. Use a black marker to draw lines across the craft stick. Cut four strands of yarn long enough to stretch across the length of the craft stick. Glue them to the stick, leaving a small space in between each strand of yarn. Cut the handle and other embellishments, as shown, out of black construction paper and glue them into place. Use a silver marker to draw in details.

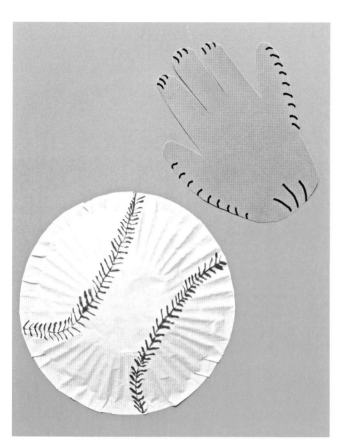

CUPCAKE LINER BASEBALL

You can also choose to use brown paint and dip your hand in to make a handprint baseball glove.

SUPPLIES

- Red and black marker
- White cupcake liner
- Construction paper
- Glue stick

DIRECTIONS

Draw baseball stitching on a cupcake liner in red marker. Trace your hand on a piece of brown construction paper and cut it out. Use a black marker to draw stitching around the handprint so that it looks like a baseball glove. Glue the outer edge of the cupcake liner and press just the outer edge to a separate piece of construction paper so that the center of the liner protrudes out. Glue the glove next to the ball.

CUPCAKE LINER BUMBLEBEE

This would be a great spring or summer craft. Make a ladybug using a red cupcake liner or a colorful spider.

SUPPLIES

- Glue stick
- Yellow cupcake liner
- Black and blue construction paper
- Black marker
- Googly eye

DIRECTIONS

Glue the yellow cupcake liner to a piece of blue construction paper. Draw vertical black lines across the yellow liner with a black marker. Cut a circle out for the head and a triangle for the stinger. Glue them into place. Glue on a googly eye. Draw the antennae on the top of the head to finish it off.

CUPCAKE LINER CLOWN

Add a jumbo craft stick to the bottom of the paper plate to make a clown mask.

SUPPLIES

- Tacky glue
- Extra-large red pom-pom
- Paper plate
- Large googly eyes
- Pink and red construction paper
- Cupcake liners (rainbow colors)

DIRECTIONS

Glue the red pom-pom to the center of the plate for the clown's nose. Glue the googly eyes above the pom-pom. Cut a mouth out of the red construction paper and glue it under the pom-pom nose. Cut out two pink circles for cheeks and glue them to the side of the pom-pom nose. Glue the spectrum of cupcake liners along the top half of the paper plate to form the clown's hair.

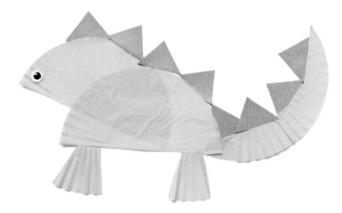

CUPCAKE LINER LIZARD

Shift the shapes around a bit and you can create a dinosaur instead.

SUPPLIES

- Green cupcake liners
- Glue stick
- Construction paper
- Googly eye

DIRECTIONS

Cut a green cupcake liner in half. Glue one of the halves at a slant with the round side facing upward to form the head. Glue and overlap a little bit more than half of that liner with another liner placed horizontally across it, round side up. Cut a tail and legs out of another cupcake liner and glue them into place. Cut a bunch of small triangles out of any color construction paper. Glue the triangles along the top of the head, body, and tail. Add a googly eye to the head.

CUPCAKE LINER PIG

If you are looking for a quick and easy craft, this little piggy is perfect and adorable.

SUPPLIES

- Tacky glue
- Pink cupcake liner
- Construction paper
- Pink buttons (one large, one medium)
- Googly eyes
- Markers

DIRECTIONS

Glue the cupcake liner to a piece of construction paper. Glue a large pink button to the center of the liner and then glue a smaller pink one into the larger button. Glue a set of googly eyes over the buttons. Cut the ears and legs out of the pink construction paper. Use markers to draw in a mouth and a squiggly tail.

CUPCAKE LINER PUP

Add spots, patches of color, or a dog collar to make this pup your own.

SUPPLIES

- Glue stick
- Cupcake liners
- Construction paper
- Large googly eyes
- Black marker

DIRECTIONS

Glue any color of cupcake liner to the top of a piece of construction paper for your head. Glue another liner in the same color directly under it for the body. Cut another cupcake liner in half and glue the halves to the sides of the head to form ears. Cut a liner into quarters and then position and glue each quarter around the sides of the body to form arms and legs. Glue large googly eyes onto the top liner. Cut a nose and a tongue out of construction paper and glue beneath the googly eyes. Use a black marker to draw in any details.

CUPCAKE LINER SCARECROW

Add a flower to the hat or add longer hair to your scarecrow to make a lady scarecrow.

SUPPLIES

- White cupcake liner
- Glue stick
- Construction paper
- Yarn
- Marker
- Large button
- Large googly eyes
- Jumbo craft stick

DIRECTIONS

Flatten out a white cupcake liner and glue it to a piece of construction paper. Cut several strands of yarn. Glue the strands of yarn along the top of the cupcake liner, jutting out in all directions. Glue more strands under the liner. Cut a hat out of construction paper. Cut a square out of a different colored piece of construction paper. Make hash marks around it using a marker and glue it onto your hat to form a patch or two. Glue a button to the center of the liner to form the nose. Glue the googly eyes above the nose and finish off your scarecrow by drawing him or her a mouth. Glue a craft stick underneath the head for the body.

CUPCAKE LINER SEASHELLS

These happy little seashells love the beach. Draw a beach pail and shovel on your beach or glue a bit of real sand to your beach backdrop.

SUPPLIES

- Cupcake liners
- Glue stick
- Googly eyes
- Marker
- Blue and tan construction paper

DIRECTIONS

Fold a cupcake liner in half. Fold another one into quarters and then glue it underneath the half liner. Glue a set of googly eyes to the half liner and then draw in a smile underneath it. Cut a piece of blue construction paper into a wavy pattern and glue it onto a piece of tan paper to form a beach. Form more cupcake liner seashells and glue them to your beachy backdrop.

CUPCAKE LINER SUBMARINE

You can use tissue paper to create underwater plant life or draw in some little fish to swim around your submarine.

SUPPLIES

- Yellow cupcake liner
- Tacky glue
- Blue construction paper
- Yellow foam
- Blue foam
- Buttons

DIRECTIONS

Flatten and glue a yellow cupcake liner to a piece of blue construction paper. Cut a yellow piece of foam into a trapezoid and two narrow ovals. Glue the trapezoid to the top of your liner and the ovals into a "V" shape coming out of the back. Cut a propeller and a scope out of the blue foam and glue the scope to the top of the trapezoid and then glue the propeller between the two yellow ovals. Glue medium to large buttons to the cupcake liner to form the portholes.

CUPCAKE LINER SUNFLOWER

You can also use real sunflower seeds or dry beans for the inside of your cupcake liners instead of buttons.

SUPPLIES

- Yellow cupcake liner
- Tacky glue
- Blue construction paper
- Brown buttons
- Green pipe cleaners

DIRECTIONS

Flip your liner inside out so that the colored side of the cupcake liner is facing upward. Snip equal cuts all around the sides of the cupcake liner. Glue the liner to the top center of a piece of blue construction paper. Glue small brown buttons into the middle of the cupcake liner. Glue a pipe cleaner under the liner for the stem and twist another pipe cleaner into a bow shape for the leaves.

CUPCAKE LINER TRACTOR

Mini cupcake liners make great wheels for any mode of transportation.

SUPPLIES

- Construction paper
- Glue stick
- Mini cupcake liner
- Regular cupcake liner
- Markers

DIRECTIONS

Cut two large rectangles out of a piece of construction paper in any color. Cut two small rectangles out of blue or white construction paper for the windows. Cut one long, narrow rectangle about half the size of the large rectangles out of another piece of construction paper. Glue one of the large rectangles horizontally to a piece of construction paper. Glue the other large rectangle vertically overlapping one of the upper corners of your horizontal shape. Glue the mini cupcake liner to the front of the horizontal rectangle and glue the larger cupcake liner to the bottom of the vertical rectangle. Glue the long narrow piece to the top center of the horizontal rectangle. Use markers to draw in smoke, grates, or any other details.

CUPCAKE LINER LILY PADS

You could make a fun little game out of this. Toss or flip your button frog and try to land it on a lily pad.

SUPPLIES

- White and green cupcake liners
- Glue stick
- Blue construction paper
- Tacky glue
- Optional: large and small green buttons, green foam, googly eyes

DIRECTIONS

Cut a pie-sized piece out of a few green cupcake liners. Glue the cupcake liners to a piece of blue construction paper. Snip lines around the edge toward the center of a few white cupcake liners. Do not cut all the way through. Pinch and fold the center of the cut white cupcake liners together so that the cut pieces stick up and form what looks like a flower. Use the glue stick to glue the cupcake liner flowers around your lily pads. If you would like to make a frog, as shown, select a large green button and a small green button, preferably in the same color. Use the tacky glue to glue the small button to the large button for the body and the head. Cut legs out of a piece of green foam and glue them to the large button. Glue on the googly eyes at the end to finish off your little frog.

CHAPTER SEVEN

PAINTING PROJECTS

Painting doesn't just have to be with brushes.
There are so many different techniques and tools that you can use.

Craft #1: Mixed Media Jungle

Craft #2: Abstract Self-Portrait

Craft #3: Crumpled Tissue Painting

Craft #4: Nature Printing

Craft #5: Paint Blot Painting

Craft #6: Painted Rocks

Craft #7: Painted Shape Flower

Craft #8: Shadow Painting

Craft #9: Shape Paintings

Craft #10: Sponge-Painted Leaves

Craft #11: Styrofoam Printing

Craft #12: Sunset Painting with Silhouette

Craft #13: Tape Resist Night Canvas

Craft #14: Textured Ombré Canvas

Craft #15: Tinfoil Embossed Painting

Craft #16: Yarn-Wrapped Canvas Painting

MIXED MEDIA JUNGLE

Combining different materials to form a single piece of artwork is challenging and fun for a creative little mind.

SUPPLIES

- Craft stick
- Green and brown acrylic paint
- Watercolor paper
- Fan and round brush
- Green cupcake liners
- Glue stick
- Black marker
- Green yarn

DIRECTIONS

Dip the side of a craft stick into brown paint, covering the whole edge. Press the stick onto a piece of paper to form branches all over. Use a fan brush and lightly dip into different shades of greens and use the side of the brush to create fanned leaves around the branches and at the bottom of the page for grass. Let the paint dry. Cut cupcake liners in half and in quarters and glue above the grass to form large jungle leaves. Use a marker to draw in veins for the leaves. Glue the green yarn in upside-down arches along the top to create vines.

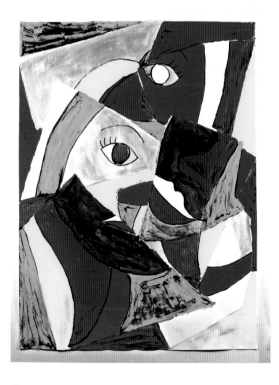

ABSTRACT SELF-PORTRAIT

Here is a fabulous opportunity to explore abstract art and maybe introduce them to some famous abstract artists and their work.

SUPPLIES

- Marker
- Watercolor paper
- Glue stick
- Acrylic paint

DIRECTIONS

Draw a self-portrait with a marker onto a piece of watercolor paper. Cut the portrait into a bunch of smaller pieces and glue the pieces randomly onto another piece of watercolor paper. It is okay if the pieces overlap. After all the pieces are glued on, paint the pieces in different colors within the dark lines and edges of your cutouts.

CRUMPLED TISSUE PAINTING

This is a lovely technique that would be great to use if making a textured backdrop to a painting, for leaves, or for a simple process art piece.

SUPPLIES

- Tissue paper
- Tempura or acrylic paint
- Watercolor paper

DIRECTIONS

Crumple up a piece of tissue paper. Dip the crumpled paper into the paint and press onto a piece of watercolor paper. Stamp the paint-covered tissue paper all around the paper. Switch colors and rotate the paper around to reveal a different texture for your stamp.

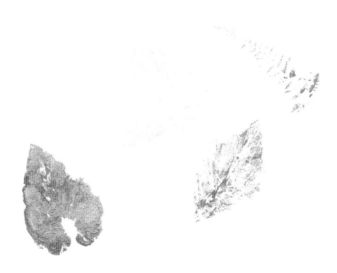

NATURE PRINTING

Nature prints are both beautiful and inexpensive to make. Try printing with rocks, flowers, or ferns.

SUPPLIES

- Acrylic paint
- Assorted leaves
- White construction paper

DIRECTIONS

Paint the backside of the leaf. Press the leaf onto a piece of paper. Press your fingers all around the leaf to make sure that all of the color transfers to the paper. Try different colors and leaves.

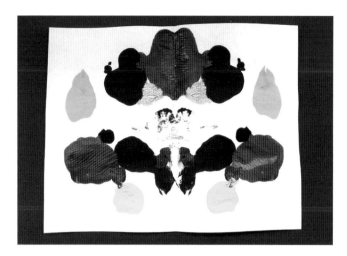

PAINT BLOT PAINTING

Make a bunch of these and challenge family and friends to describe what they see in your blots.

SUPPLIES
- White paper
- Tempura or acrylic paints

DIRECTIONS

Fold a piece of paper in half. Open the paper back up and splatter or squeeze globs of paint around your paper, careful not to get too close to the edges. Refold the paper and smooth it out with your hand. Open it back up and check out your paint blot.

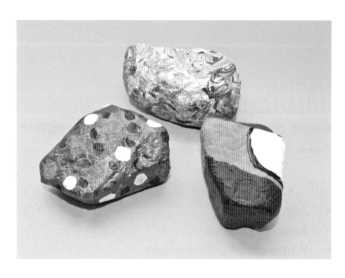

PAINTED ROCKS

Nature painting is so much fun, and the best part is gathering your supplies. Nature painting is not limited to rocks. Paint flower petals, leaves, acorns, or pinecones. They all make wonderful canvases.

SUPPLIES
- Rocks
- Acrylic paint
- Optional: glitter

DIRECTIONS

Wash your rocks first to get off any dirt or debris. Paint your rocks however you choose. Paint them solid colors, paint them with a design, or paint your name or a picture on them. Add glitter to your wet paint to make pretty glittery gemstones.

PAINTED SHAPE FLOWER

There are no rules for painting your flower shapes. Choose any color or pattern. This would be a great project for even your smallest little finger painter with assistance from an adult.

SUPPLIES

- Tempura or acrylic paint
- White paper
- Glue stick
- Pipe cleaner

DIRECTIONS

You can choose to paint the whole paper first and then cut out the circle for the center of your flower, petals, and leaves, or you can cut out all the shapes first and then paint them all individually. Let the paint dry and then glue the shapes to a piece of paper to form the flower. Use a pipe cleaner for the stem or simply paint one on.

SHADOW PAINTING

This is a wonderful art project that can be done both outdoors and indoors. You can find a natural shadow or create your own using blocks or other props.

SUPPLIES

- A shadow of anything
- Watercolor paper
- Watercolors

DIRECTIONS

This is really easy to set up. First, all you have to do is find or create a shadow using various objects. We chose a flower outdoors, but this can be done with building blocks and other assorted items as well. Place a piece of watercolor paper in the line of your shadow. Use watercolors to paint in your shadow.

SHAPE PAINTINGS

This is a simple and fun piece of abstract art.

SUPPLIES

- Cookie cutter shape or cardboard
- Canvas or watercolor paper
- Black Sharpie
- Acrylic paint

DIRECTIONS

Cookie cutters will work great for this, but you can also cut a shape out of cardboard and use it as a template. Pick a shape or a few of your choosing. Place the shapes on your paper and outline them with the Sharpie. Move the shape around the paper, overlapping other shapes, and keep outlining until you have covered all around your paper. Paint within the Sharpie lines in different colors to make a cool piece of shape art.

SPONGE-PAINTED LEAVES

Sponges make wonderful stamps for painting. Try different shapes or objects.

SUPPLIES

- Sponges
- Brown and white construction paper
- Acrylic paint

DIRECTIONS

Cut different leaf shapes out of sponges. To make the tree, cut a tree trunk and branches out of brown construction paper. Glue it to a piece of white construction paper. Dip the sponge into the paint and press the different shapes around the branches. Change the colors around or mix the color on the same leaf for multicolored leaves.

STYROFOAM PRINTING

Stamping and printing are a fun way to explore paint, and styrofoam printing is simple and fun.

SUPPLIES

- Styrofoam plate
- Tempura paint or acrylics
- White paper

DIRECTIONS

Use a blunt-tipped pencil and draw a picture or design into a Styrofoam plate by pressing it into the Styrofoam so that it leaves an indented image. Dip the plate into the paint or paint over the plate and then press onto a piece of paper to reveal the design.

SUNSET PAINTING WITH SILHOUETTE

This is a craft project for all ages or skill levels.

SUPPLIES

- Watercolor paints (red, orange, yellow, purple)
- Watercolor paper
- Black construction paper
- Glue

DIRECTIONS

Use red, orange, yellow, and purple paints to paint your piece of watercolor paper. There are no rules for how you would like to paint this. Paint in swirls, lines, or just splatter on the paint. Set the picture aside to let the paint dry. Cut a simple sailboat shape out of black construction paper and add a wave or two if you would like, as well. Glue the silhouettes over the painting once the paint has dried.

TAPE RESIST NIGHT CANVAS

Tape resist is a clever way to create an interesting piece of artwork. Your tape can be completely abstract or form specific shapes such as in this one.

SUPPLIES

- Masking tape
- Painting canvas
- Acrylic paint

DIRECTIONS

Tear off strips of tape and overlap them slightly side by side to form a larger surface of tape. Cut a star shape out of this. Do this again with the tape and cut out a moon crescent. Tape both the star and the moon onto the canvas. Use additional strips to accent your painting or form more stars or planets. Make sure that your tape is secure and then paint over the tape in purples, blacks, and blues for your night sky. When the paint is dry, pull off your tape and reveal your masterpiece.

TEXTURED OMBRÉ CANVAS

I love the look of pointillism, but it can be a tedious process for little fingers. This textured process gives the look of pointillism in a fun, quick way. The ombré is a great way to explore color mixing and blending.

SUPPLIES

- Cotton swabs
- Rubber band
- Acrylic paint
- Painting palette
- Painting canvas

DIRECTIONS

Bundle a handful of cotton swabs together and bind together with a rubber band. Make sure that the swabs are flush on the ends. Select just a couple of colors that will blend nicely together. Squeeze the paints onto a palette. Add white to your palette, as well. Pull colors from one area on your palette and bring them to another area and mix them with white to lighten the shades. Lighten it several times to form new colors. Dip your bunched swabs into the lightest shade of paint that you formed. Start at the edge of your canvas and dab all the way across. Repeat using the next darkest shade of the same color and dabbing above the first line of color. Continue until you get to your darkest shade in that color. When you get to the darkest shade, mix your two color choices together to blend them and then dab with that color. Move into the next color and continue dabbing across until you reach the other end.

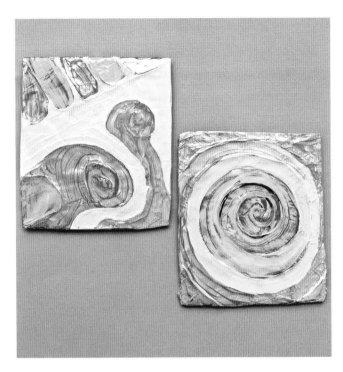

TINFOIL EMBOSSED PAINTING

There are actually a few different methods that you can try for this. Try them all or the one that works best for you.

SUPPLIES
- Cardboard
- Yarn, tacky glue, or low-temperature glue gun
- Tinfoil
- Acrylic paint

DIRECTIONS

Cut a shape out of a piece of cardboard. There are a few methods that you can choose. Pick the one that you think works best.

Method 1: Squeeze out a design with either tacky glue or a low-temperature glue gun and let it dry.

Method 2: Make a design by forming shapes with yarn and gluing it down.

Once you have completed the selected method, place a piece of tinfoil over your design and fold under. Smooth the foil out over the design so that the design is raised in the foil. Paint around your design and let dry.

YARN-WRAPPED CANVAS PAINTING

Here is a different form of resist art that is fun and easy to do and has an element of fine motor skills to it, as well.

SUPPLIES

- Yarn
- Paint canvas
- Clothespin
- Cotton ball
- Acrylic paint

DIRECTIONS

Wrap yarn around a piece of canvas. Wrap the yarn around snugly and in every direction. Use a clothespin to hold a cotton ball. Use the cotton ball to dab paint around the canvas. Dabbing the paint will ensure that you do not drag paint under the yarn. Let the paint dry completely and then unravel or cut away the yarn to reveal your design.

CHAPTER EIGHT

PIPE CLEANERS

With the way pipe cleaners bend and form, they are
a crafting dream. Bend, twist, string, and fold
your pipe cleaners to find inspiration.

Craft #1: Glittery Pipe Cleaner Butterfly

Craft #2: Pipe Cleaner Creepy Crawlers

Craft #3: Pipe Cleaner Dragonfly

Craft #4: Pipe Cleaner Drawings

Craft #5: Pipe Cleaner Lion

Craft #6: Pipe Cleaner Roses

Craft #7: Pipe Cleaner Spider

Craft #8: Pipe Cleaner Stethoscope

Craft #9: Pipe Cleaner Sun

Craft #10: Pipe Cleaner Tic-Tac-Toe

Craft #11: Pipe Cleaner Tree

Craft #12: Pufferfish

Craft #13: Pipe Cleaner Weaving

Craft #14: Pipe Cleaner X-Ray

Craft #15: Swinging Monkeys

Craft #16: Wacky Arm Aliens

GLITTERY PIPE CLEANER BUTTERFLY

You can also glue tissue paper to the wax paper and tie a string to these to hang in the window for a pretty suncatching ornament.

SUPPLIES
- Pipe cleaners
- Tacky glue
- Wax paper
- Glitter

DIRECTIONS

Curve one pipe cleaner to form the shape of a butterfly wing and then curve another the exact same way. Coil and wrap another pipe cleaner around the two wings to join them together. Cut a pipe cleaner in half, fold it into a "V," and curl slightly at the end to form the antennae. Glue it to the top center of the butterfly. Glue the butterfly to a piece of wax paper and let the glue dry. Cut the wax paper around the butterfly shape. Use glue to squeeze out designs onto the wax paper. Sprinkle glitter over the glue and let it sit to dry. Shake off the excess glitter once the glue has dried.

PIPE CLEANER CREEPY CRAWLERS

The coils on the insects make them extra squirmy and wiggly.

SUPPLIES

- Pipe cleaners
- Tacky glue or low-temperature glue gun
- Googly eyes
- Craft pom-pom

ANT

DIRECTIONS

Coil two black pipe cleaners. Coil one tighter and one looser. Insert the looser coil into the tighter coil. Glue googly eyes to the tighter coil. Cut a piece of pipe cleaner to form the antennae. Cut three equal sections of black pipe cleaner and form legs using the same method as with the caterpillar.

CATERPILLAR

DIRECTIONS

Coil several different colored pipe cleaners around your finger to form spirals. Tuck the spirals into each other one at a time to form a long segmented coil. Glue a small set of googly eyes to a pom-pom and then fold one-third of a black pipe cleaner in half and glue it to the top of the pom-pom to form the antennae. Let the glue dry and then glue the pom-pom to the front of the coil for the head. Cut a black pipe cleaner in several short equal-length pieces for the legs. Loop them around the segments and curve down to form small legs. Add glue where each coil is inserted to hold into place more securely.

PIPE CLEANER DRAGONFLY

Twisting and curling pipe cleaners is great for working on those fine motor skills.

SUPPLIES

- Pipe cleaners
- Tacky glue or low-temperature glue gun
- Large button
- Googly eyes

DIRECTIONS

Make a loop with a pipe cleaner in any color to form a wing. Repeat this step again with another pipe cleaner. Cut a little piece off of two more pipe cleaners and form a smaller set of wings. Use another pipe cleaner to wrap around the two sets of wings so that they are joined together with the larger set of wings on top of the smaller set. Let the other end of that pipe cleaner hang down. Fold and twist the end upward to form the dragonfly's tail. Glue a large button above the large wings and add googly eyes to form the head.

PIPE CLEANER DRAWINGS

It was my four year old that came up with this idea, as she loves making pipe cleaner people and animals.

SUPPLIES

- Pipe cleaners
- Tacky glue

DIRECTIONS

Cut different colored pipe cleaners into different lengths. Twist, bend, and form pictures and designs using the pipe cleaners. Glue the pieces down to save your artwork.

PIPE CLEANER LION

Coil even more pipe cleaners to make a fuller mane for your king of the jungle.

SUPPLIES

- Egg carton
- Yellow acrylic paint
- Yellow foam
- Low-temperature glue gun
- Yellow pipe cleaners
- Googly eyes
- Black marker

DIRECTIONS

Paint one section of the egg carton in yellow paint. Let the paint dry. Cut two small ears out of a piece of yellow foam. Hold the egg carton so that it is like a rounded diamond. Glue the ears on either side of the top rounded point with the glue gun. Curl two or more pipe cleaners around your finger to make spirals. Curve the spirals around the egg carton and glue into place. Glue the googly eyes onto the top of the egg carton underneath the ears. Use a marker to draw in the nose, mouth, and whiskers.

PIPE CLEANER ROSES

For a simpler rose, just make a loose coil without weaving in the petals; the rose effect will still be there. These would be a great craft for Mother's Day or Valentine's Day.

SUPPLIES

- Red pipe cleaners
- Green pipe cleaners

DIRECTIONS

Coil one of the red pipe cleaners to form the center of your flower. Weave and curve petals around the center coil. Curve as many pipe cleaners as you would like to achieve your desired flower. Stick a green pipe cleaner up the back of the flower and curl the end to hold in place. Form a bow shape with another green pipe cleaner for the leaves.

PIPE CLEANER SPIDER

Pipe cleaners make creepy legs for your favorite creepy crawlers.

SUPPLIES

- Egg carton
- Acrylic paint
- Tacky glue or low-temperature glue gun

- Pipe cleaners
- Googly eyes
- Black marker

DIRECTIONS

Cut three sections of the egg carton and then paint them in the color of your choice. Let the paint dry. Glue two of the egg carton pieces together at their open ends and then glue the remaining piece sideways to the two glued pieces. Cut three pipe cleaners in any color in half and bend and form them into legs and then glue them underneath the egg carton pieces. Glue on a pair of googly eyes and draw a happy face for your friendly spider.

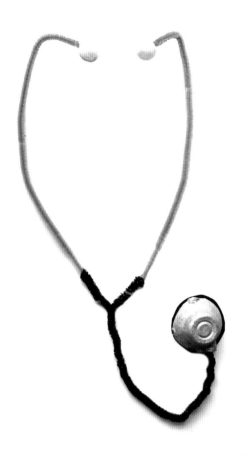

PIPE CLEANER STETHOSCOPE

What do your kids want to be when they grow up? If they have ever thought of becoming doctors or nurses, as many little boys and girls do, this is a great project that can be used for a little pretend play.

SUPPLIES

- Pipe cleaners
- Low-temperature glue gun or tacky glue
- Pom-poms
- Egg carton (round preferred)
- Acrylic paint
- Foam sheet

DIRECTIONS

Select two pipe cleaners in the same color. Bend one end of each about 1 inch. Glue a small pom-pom to the bent end on each. Choose two more pipe cleaners in a different color. Twist together, leaving one end untwisted and open in the shape of a "Y." Twist each end of the "Y" into the unbent ends of the first set of pipe cleaners. Cut a piece of egg carton and paint it. Let the paint dry. Cut a piece of foam to fit under the egg carton. Glue the egg carton and foam shape together around the tip of the twisted pipe cleaners so that it hangs from the bottom. Let the glue dry and then your stethoscope is ready to use.

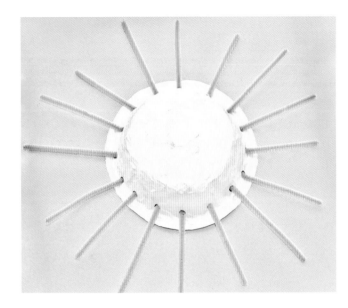

PIPE CLEANER SUN

Let the kids tear up the pieces of tissue paper for a little added fun instead of cutting the pieces. They will love being able to rip up the paper into small pieces.

SUPPLIES

- Yellow tissue paper
- School glue
- Paper bowl
- Hole punch
- Yellow pipe cleaners

DIRECTIONS

Tear yellow tissue paper into small pieces. Squeeze the glue on your paper bowl and use a paintbrush to spread it around. Place the tissue pieces over the glue. Overlap pieces and use more glue as needed. Let the glue and paper dry. Use a hole punch to punch holes around the bottom of the bowl, just above the lip of the bowl. Insert the pipe cleaners into holes on one end and have them exit through holes on the other. Continue until you fill all of the holes with pipe cleaners.

PIPE CLEANER TIC-TAC-TOE

Tic-Tac-Toe is a wonderful game that teaches children about planning and strategy. This board can be made and used over and over again.

SUPPLIES

- Pipe cleaners
- Small poster board
- Tacky blue or low-temperature glue gun

DIRECTIONS

Lay four full-sized pipe cleaners in any color onto a piece of small poster board. Glue two across horizontally and then lay two across vertically to form a hash mark. Cut three pipe cleaners in a different color in half and bend each section into a circle. Twist to hold the circle in place. Form five circles. Cut three more pipe cleaners in another color in half. Cut each of those in half again and twist the two quarters into an "X." Form five X's. Enjoy your new game.

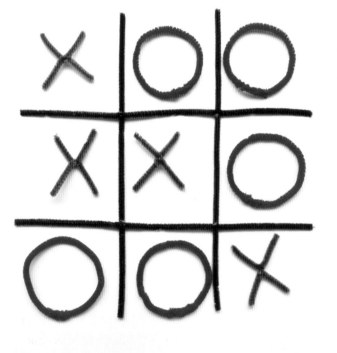

PIPE CLEANER TREE

This pipe cleaner tree can change with the seasons, as well. Switch the green pipe cleaners for fall colored pipe cleaners for autumn, use white pipe cleaners for the winters, and shake on sparkly white glitter or use green pipe cleaners with pink tissue or pom-poms glued on for the spring.

SUPPLIES

- Toilet paper roll
- Brown acrylic paint
- Hole punch
- Green pipe cleaners

DIRECTIONS

Paint the toilet paper roll brown and let it dry. Use a hole punch to punch holes around one end of the toilet paper roll. Stagger your holes at different levels. Insert one end of a pipe cleaner into one of the holes and loop the pipe cleaner over to a hole on the opposite end of the toilet paper roll. Continue to do this with the pipe cleaners until all holes are filled. You may use more than one pipe cleaner in a hole, as well.

PUFFERFISH

This is a cute bit of fine motor play with clay.

SUPPLIES

- Yellow polymer clay
- Googly eyes
- Yellow pipe cleaners

DIRECTIONS

Roll a chunk of clay into a ball as large as you would like your fish. Form two little fins with the clay and mold them to the side of the ball. Stick a couple of googly eyes into the clay at the top of the ball and poke a hole for a mouth below it using a pencil. Cut pipe cleaners into equal-sized pieces about 1½ inches long. Stick the pipe cleaners into the ball, avoiding the face and the fins.

PIPE CLEANER WEAVING

This is a great activity to sharpen fine motor skills and to learn movement patterns.

SUPPLIES

- Hole punch
- Paper plate
- Pipe cleaners

DIRECTIONS

Use the hole punch to punch holes about a ½ inch apart all around the outside of your paper plate. Poke a pipe cleaner through the bottom of one of the holes and all the way across the top of the plate and down a hole on the opposite end. Fold the ends of the pipe cleaner down to hold it in place. Run more pipe cleaners parallel to the first, skipping every other hole. Rotate the plate and insert a pipe cleaner into a hole going perpendicular to the others, but this time weave under and over the existing pipe cleaners. Repeat this across, again skipping every other hole. Rotate the plate and weave from the other end. Continue this process until you are satisfied with your weave.

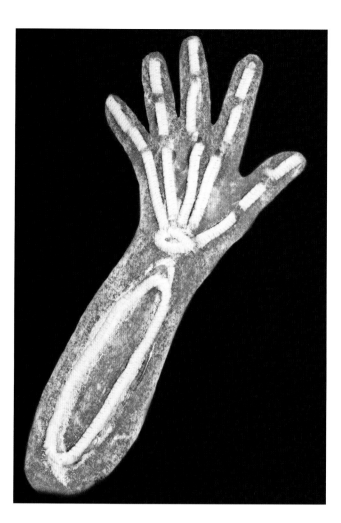

PIPE CLEANER X-RAY

The child can also cover their arm and hand in white paint and press onto black paper to make their x-ray arm.

SUPPLIES

- Black construction paper
- White chalk
- White pipe cleaners
- Tacky glue

DIRECTIONS

Trace your hand and arm onto a piece of black construction paper. Lightly dust the cutout in white chalk. Cut out the tracing. Cut sections of pipe cleaner to form the hand and arm bones. Glue the pipe cleaner segments in place and let dry. Glue the whole thing to another piece of black construction paper.

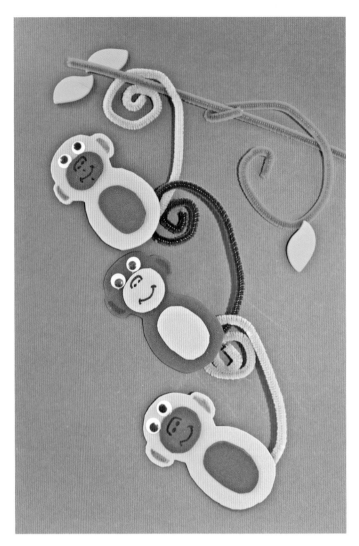

SWINGING MONKEYS

These fun little swinging monkeys love hanging around the house. They will happily dangle in your child's room or a classroom.

SUPPLIES

- Foam sheets
- Tacky glue
- Googly eyes
- Pink and black markers
- Pipe cleaners

DIRECTIONS

Sketch the shape of a monkey onto a piece of foam sheet. Cut out the shape. Cut a small circle and an oval out of a different colored foam sheet. Make the shapes small enough to fit into each rounded section of the body. Glue the small circle onto the top head portion of your monkey's body. Glue the oval onto the lower body portion. Glue googly eyes to the top of the circular portion of your monkey body. Use a pink marker to color in the inner ears and use a black marker to draw in facial details. Curl about one-third or one-half of a pipe cleaner with your finger. Glue the uncurled end to the back of your monkey toward the bottom of the oval end of your body. Let the glue dry completely. Make several and let them hang from one another's tails.

WACKY ARM ALIENS

Anything goes with these wacky aliens. Give them two arms, nine arms, two eyes or five. Use other embellishments, as well. Make a glitter alien or give your alien some yarn hair.

SUPPLIES

- Clothespins
- Acrylic paint
- Pipe cleaners
- Tacky glue
- Googly eyes
- Black markers

DIRECTIONS

Paint the clothespins in the colors of your choice. Let the clothespins dry. Bend, curl, or zigzag a pipe cleaner. Open the clothespin and insert the middle of the pipe cleaner into the clothespin. Glue on googly eyes and use markers to draw in any details.

CHAPTER NINE

POM-POM CRAFTS

With their soft and fuzzy texture, pom-poms are a fun craft material to work with.

Craft #1: Pom-Pom Birthday Cake

Craft #2: Pom-Pom Clover

Craft #3: Pom-Pom Cupcakes

Craft #4: Pom-Pom Duck

Craft #5: Pom-Pom Flamingo

Craft #6: Pom-Pom Painting

Craft #7: Pom-Pom Grapes

Craft #8: Pom-Pom Gumball Machine

Craft #9: Pom-Pom Igloo

Craft #10: Pom-Pom Insects

Craft #11: Pom-Pom Pinecone Ornament

Craft #12: Pom-Pom Owl

Craft #13: Pom-Pom UFO

Craft #14: Pom-Pom Wreath

Craft #15: Pom-Pom Traffic Light

POM-POM BIRTHDAY CAKE

Birthday cake is fun to eat, but it is even more fun to decorate. Use pom-poms, foam stickers, plastic flowers, or even sequins.

SUPPLIES

- Construction paper
- School glue
- Pipe cleaners
- Pom-poms
- Foam flower stickers
- Markers

DIRECTIONS

Cut round cake shapes in three different sizes out of construction paper in any color. Glue your tiers to another piece of construction paper, gluing your largest tier to the bottom and stacking upward from largest to smallest. Cut 1-inch pieces of pipe cleaner to form candles, and use pom-poms, flower shapes, and markers to decorate your cake.

POM-POM CLOVER

Make an extra leaf for a little extra luck.

SUPPLIES

- Green pipe cleaners
- Tacky glue
- Green pom-poms

DIRECTIONS

Form a small loop on the end of a pipe cleaner. Roll another loop from the other end next to it, and loop the end of the pipe cleaner around the middle of the two circles. Form another loop the same size as the other loops with another pipe cleaner. Center it between the other two loops and join it to the other loops by wrapping the pipe cleaner around the center of the original two loops. Pull the loose end below the two loops to form your stem. Glue a pom-pom in the middle of each loop.

POM-POM CUPCAKES

These are fun and easy to make and are perfect for pretend play. Make a whole bakery or have a play bake sale with these adorable pom-pom cupcakes.

SUPPLIES

- Craft pom-poms (extra-large and small)
- Mini cupcake liners
- Tacky glue
- Optional: buttons, foam sheets, pipe cleaners, gemstones, sequins

DIRECTIONS

Place an extra-large pom-pom in a mini cupcake liner. Glue other tiny pom-poms, buttons, sequins, cut-up foam sheets, or whatever else you can think of to your cupcakes to decorate them.

POM-POM DUCK

The pom-poms make for a soft and fluffy duck.

SUPPLIES

- Yellow and white construction paper
- Tacky glue
- Yellow pom-poms
- Orange foam
- Googly eye

DIRECTIONS

Sketch and cut out a duck body shape using a piece of yellow construction paper. Glue the duck's shape to a piece of white construction paper. Cover the yellow shape with yellow pom-poms. Cut a beak and legs out of orange foam and glue them in place, and finish off your craft with a googly eye.

POM-POM FLAMINGO

This flamingo is pretty in pink. Add a few pink gemstones or sequins to give this already vibrant bird a little more pizazz.

SUPPLIES

- Pink and white construction paper
- School glue
- Pink pipe cleaners
- Pink pom-poms
- Pink feathers
- Googly eye
- Black marker

DIRECTIONS

Cut a large circle out of a piece of pink construction paper. Cut the flaimingo's curvy neck and head out of the pink paper, as well. Glue the circle to the center of the paper and then glue the neck and head to the side of the circle. Cut a pipe cleaner in half and bend one of the halves in half. Glue both pipe cleaners under the circle to form the legs. Glue pink pom-poms to the circle and glue feathers coming out of the back end of the circle. Finish off your flamingo by gluing a googly eye to the head and coloring in the beak with a black marker.

POM-POM PAINTING

This is a simple bit of process art perfect for children of all ages.

SUPPLIES

- Pom-poms in different sizes
- Clothespins
- Acrylic paint or tempura paint
- Canvas or thick paper

DIRECTIONS

Select a variety of pom-poms in different sizes. Pinch a clothespin around each pom-pom. Dip the pom-poms into the paint and just have fun with it. Dot, swipe, streak, or pat your pom-poms across your canvas or paper. Enjoy.

POM-POM GRAPES

Grapes don't just have to be purple. Use green or red pom-poms to make your favorite kind of grape.

SUPPLIES

- White and green construction paper
- School glue
- Purple pom-poms
- Green pipe cleaners
- Black marker

DIRECTIONS

Cut a stem and leaves out of a piece of green construction paper. Glue to the top of a white piece of construction paper. Glue the purple pom-poms underneath the stem and leaves. You may choose to do this with green pom-poms, as well. Curl a couple of green pipe cleaners with your finger and glue them near the top to form vines. Use a marker to draw the veins into the leaves.

POM-POM GUMBALL MACHINE

Brightly colored buttons or painted thumbprints would also make a sweet alternative for making gumballs.

SUPPLIES

- Red cupcake liner
- School glue
- Construction paper
- Small pom-poms
- Black marker

DIRECTIONS

Cut both sides off of a red cupcake liner at a slight slant. Glue the cut liner to the bottom half of a piece of construction paper with the wider part of the liner facing downward. Glue a full red liner overlapping the top of the cut liner. Glue different colored pom-poms to the top cupcake liner, just leaving a little bit of the liner showing on the outer edge. Use a marker to draw in the details for your gumball machine.

POM-POM IGLOO

There is something magical about snow and ice. All of that white is so beautiful. Cover your igloo in cotton for a snowier feel.

SUPPLIES

- Toilet paper tube
- Paper bowl
- Tacky glue
- Small white and light blue pom-poms

DIRECTIONS

Cut a toilet paper tube in half and then cut the long way so it opens up. Spread out the opening so it forms an arch. Cut an opening the size of the arch out of the paper bowl. Glue the tube into the opening so that about an inch protrudes from the plate. Let the glue dry. Spread glue over your bowl, working in small sections, and glue on the white and blue pom-poms. Do the same with the toilet paper tube.

POM-POM INSECTS

What is it about bugs that kids love so much? These fuzzy creepy crawlers are perfect for your little insect lovers.

SPIDER SUPPLIES

- Tacky glue or low-temperature glue gun
- Medium pom-pom (any color)
- Extra-large pom-pom (any color)
- Pipe cleaners
- Googly eyes

DIRECTIONS

Glue a medium-sized pom-pom to the side of an extra-large one to form the spider's head and body. Cut two pipe cleaners in half to give you four pieces. Curve each pipe cleaner in the middle and glue to the bottom of your extra-large pom-pom so that the pipe cleaners form eight equal-sized legs on both sides. Let your glue dry. (The low-temperature glue gun might work best for pipe cleaners.) Once the glue dries, adjust your legs to how you would like them. Glue the googly eyes onto the head.

LADYBUG SUPPLIES

- Tacky glue
- Medium black pom-pom
- Extra-large red pom-pom
- Black foam
- Small black pom-poms
- Googly eyes

DIRECTIONS

Position and glue a medium-sized black pom-pom to the top of an extra-large red pom-pom to form a head and a body for your ladybug. Glue it off to the side, not centered. Cut two half circles out of the foam and then glue them onto the red pom-pom to form a "V" shape. Glue a few small black pom-poms around the red pom-pom. Glue the googly eyes onto the head.

POM-POM PINECONE ORNAMENT

Whether you find them in your backyard or buy them in the store, pinecones are great fun. They are perfect for fine motor crafting and fun. You may also try wrapping your pinecones in yarn or string.

SUPPLIES

- Pinecone
- Pom-poms
- Yarn
- Glitter
- School glue

DIRECTIONS

You may paint your pinecone or leave it natural. Stuff a pinecone with differently sized and colored pom-poms. Glue a loop of yarn to the top of the pinecone and cover the glue point with a ring of pom-poms. Drip glue around the pinecone or line the glue around the edges. Shake glitter all over it and let it dry. Shake the excess glitter off.

POM-POM OWL

This little pom-pom owl looks like a miniature stuffed animal.

SUPPLIES

- Tacky glue
- Medium brown pom-pom
- Large brown pom-pom
- Black and orange foam
- Googly eyes

DIRECTIONS

Glue a medium brown pom-pom to the top of a large brown pom-pom to form the head and the body. Cut wings and the tuft of feathers for the top of the head out of a sheet of black foam and then cut the beak and feet out of orange foam. Glue all of the foam shapes to the two pom-poms to form your owl. Add the googly eyes to finish it off.

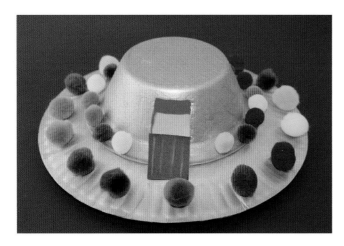

POM-POM UFO

Plastic gemstones or a combination of the gemstones and pom-poms will also work nicely to light up your UFO.

SUPPLIES
- Tacky glue
- Paper plates
- Paper or Styrofoam bowl
- Silver acrylic paint
- Small pom-poms

DIRECTIONS

Glue the tops of the paper plates together. Cut a small door shape into the bowl and bend the flap down. Glue the bowl to the top center of the paper plates. Paint the whole thing in silver and let it dry. Glue pom-poms around the bowl and plates for the UFO lights.

POM-POM WREATH

It doesn't need to be the holiday season to make this bright and colorful wreath.

SUPPLIES
- Paper plate
- Tacky glue
- Pom-poms
- Pipe cleaner or ribbon

DIRECTIONS

Cut a hole in the center of a paper plate to form a ring. Glue assorted pom-poms to the plate. Tie a pipe cleaner or a ribbon into a bow and glue to your wreath to finish it off.

POM-POM TRAFFIC LIGHT

This is a great color sorting and matching activity as well as a craft. See if the kids know what each color of the traffic light represents when they are done.

SUPPLIES

- Black, red, yellow, and green construction paper
- School glue
- Red, yellow, and green pom-poms

DIRECTIONS

Cut the base of your traffic light out of a piece of black construction paper. Cut large circles out of the red, yellow, and green construction papers and glue to the black paper with the red at the top, yellow in the middle, and the green on the bottom. Glue the correct colored pom-poms into each traffic light.

CHAPTER TEN

RECYCLABLES WITH A PURPOSE

Doesn't it always seem like your recycling bin is always filled with egg cartons, cardboard tubes, and boxes? It seems a shame to throw those away when they make such fantastic and cheap craft materials. If you can recycle it, you can probably craft with it too.

Craft #1: Bottle Cap Crabs

Craft #2: Cardboard Journal

Craft #3: Toilet Paper Tube Hammer

Craft #4: Dixie Cup Trophy

Craft #5: Egg Carton Mouse

Craft #6: Egg Carton School Bus

Craft #7: Egg Carton Swan

Craft #8: Egg Carton Teddy Bear

Craft #9: Egg Carton Watch

Craft #10: Googly Eye Goggles

Craft #11: Oat Container Piggy Bank

Craft #12: Cardboard Roll Telescope

Craft #13: Recyclable Wind Chime

Craft #14: Tissue Box Castle

Craft #15: Toilet Paper Tube Fairy Village

Craft #16: Egg Carton Cars

Craft #17: Toilet Paper Tube Airplane

BOTTLE CAP CRABS

Hold on to those old plastic bottles. The bottles and caps make for great crafts.

SUPPLIES

- Red pipe cleaners
- Tacky glue or low-temperature glue gun
- Milk caps
- Red foam
- Medium googly eyes

DIRECTIONS

Cut four equal sections of pipe cleaner large enough so that when glued to the bottom of the caps, they stick out on each end to form eight legs. You may need to bend the pipe cleaners into the cap a bit so that the glue sticks better and the cap lays flat. Cut claws out of a piece of red foam. Cut another pipe cleaner in half and glue the claws to each end of that pipe cleaner. Glue the pipe cleaner with claws to the bottom of the cap and curve the pipe cleaners forward. Glue a set of googly eyes to the cap to finish them off.

CARDBOARD JOURNAL

Create your own personal art journal or diary using old cardboard.

SUPPLIES

- Cardboard
- Hole punch
- White drawing paper
- Acrylic paint
- Tissue paper
- School glue
- Letter stickers
- Pipe cleaners

DIRECTIONS

Cut two identical rectangular pieces of cardboard. Use a hole punch to punch three holes into the top of a piece of the cardboard. Place that piece of cardboard over the other piece of cardboard as a template and mark on the other piece where the holes are. Punch holes where your marks are. Trim some white drawing paper a bit smaller than your rectangles and mark the paper for placement of your hole as well. Punch the holes in the paper and set aside. Paint the pieces of cardboard in acrylic paint and then set them aside to let them dry. Tear or cut different colored pieces of tissue paper and glue to one side of each piece of cardboard. Layer the tissue on top of each other. Let the tissue dry. Use stickers to personalize your art journal. When you are done with this, assemble your journal. Use the personalized side as your cover. Place the white paper under it, lining up the holes. Line up the holes on the other piece of cardboard for your back cover. Have the tissue side facing down. Loop three pipe cleaners through each hole and twist together to form equal-sized circles to bind your journal together.

TOILET PAPER TUBE HAMMER

It would be fun to challenge your kids to construct a whole toolbox and tools out of recyclables. You could use more tubes to make a screwdriver. Cardboard would be great to use to form a wrench and a level.

SUPPLIES

- Paper towel tube
- Acrylic paint (silver, black, and brown)
- Toilet paper tubes
- Low-temperature glue gun
- Egg carton section

DIRECTIONS

Trim a 1½ -inch section off of a paper towel tube. Paint the remainder of the paper towel tube in black and set the small section aside to use later. Cut up the length of one toilet paper tube. Reroll it back together, but overlap it a bit to make the tube narrower. Glue it into place and then paint it brown. Wrap the leftover 1½-inch section around the bottom of the brown tube and insert it into the black tube. Having that section will make the narrower brown tube fit more snugly in the wider black tube. Paint the other two toilet paper tubes in silver. Cut one of the silver tubes in half. Glue one of the silver halves to the top of the brown tube. Your handle should now be formed. To form the hammer head, cut the other silver tube lengthwise and then reroll it to make it narrower and then glue it together and insert it into the uncut silver tube. Paint the egg carton in silver and then glue it to the end of the narrower silver tube at the top. Cut two long narrow rectangular sections out of a tube and paint them silver. Glue to the back of the wider silver tube and curve it down a bit. Glue the hammer head to the top of the handle.

DIXIE CUP TROPHY

This would be a sweet gift idea for mom, dad, a grandparent, or a teacher.

SUPPLIES

- Two paper cups
- Gold and silver paint
- Tacky glue or low-temperature glue gun
- Cardboard
- Gold pipe cleaner
- White construction paper
- Black marker

DIRECTIONS

Paint the outside of the paper cups in gold and the inside in silver. Let the paint dry. Glue the two bottoms together. Cut a square of cardboard about twice as big as the paper cup. Fold the cardboard equally on either end to form a base for your trophy. Cut two small square sections to fit between the folded sections on either end to form a box. Paint your base and let it dry. Cut the pipe cleaner in half and curl the ends on each half so that one end curls in and one curls out. Make the two halves as close to the same as possible. Glue to each side of the top paper cup. The glue gun will probably work best for this part. Glue the trophy to the top of the base. Cut a rectangle out of the white paper so that it will fit onto the front of the base. Write a message with the black marker onto the paper for the special recipient.

EGG CARTON MOUSE

Make a cat with pointy ears and front paws to make a cat and mouse pair.

SUPPLIES

- Egg carton
- Yellow acrylic paint
- Yellow foam
- Pink foam
- Tacky glue
- Yellow pipe cleaner
- Googly eyes
- Pink and black markers

DIRECTIONS

Paint one section of egg carton in yellow and let it dry. Cut ears out of a piece of yellow foam and a small nose out of pink foam. Glue the ears and nose to the egg carton. Cut a piece of pipe cleaner and curl it slightly. Glue on a set of googly eyes. Draw in whiskers with a black marker and color the inside of the ears with the pink marker.

EGG CARTON SCHOOL BUS

Egg carton shapes and sizes vary. This might not work with every carton.

SUPPLIES

- Egg carton
- Yellow and black acrylic paint
- Tacky glue
- Black marker
- Red and white round gemstones
- Red construction paper
- Black pipe cleaner
- White foam

DIRECTIONS

Paint the top cover of an egg carton in yellow paint and set it aside to let it dry. It may require a few coats. Paint two of the egg carton sections in black and let them dry. Glue the egg carton sections to the front and rear of the bottom of the egg carton cover to form the wheels. Paint a black stripe across the bottom of the egg carton cover horizontally. Use a marker to write SCHOOL BUS along the top of the bus. Glue a red gemstone to the side of the back end of the bus and glue a white and a red gemstone to the front side. This will be to form the lights. Cut a stop sign out of red construction paper. Write STOP on the paper and glue toward the front above the front wheel. Cut a small section of pipe cleaner and poke each end through the area behind the first front window opening so that it is inserted vertically. Cut a small rounded rectangle out of white foam for a side mirror and glue it over the pipe cleaner.

EGG CARTON SWAN

This a simple and pretty craft. The feathers make our little swan sweet and angelic.

SUPPLIES

- Egg carton section
- White acrylic paint
- White foam
- Orange foam
- Tacky glue
- Black marker
- White feathers

DIRECTIONS

Cut a section of egg carton. Paint it white and set it aside to dry. Cut a slit into the side of the egg carton section. Cut a curvy shape for the neck and head out of white foam. Cut a small beak out of orange foam. Glue the beak onto the swan's head. Use the black marker to draw in the black markings on the swan's face. Glue the neck into the slit in the egg carton. Glue the white feathers on the egg carton section facing away from the head.

EGG CARTON TEDDY BEAR

If you are feeling extra crafty, use construction paper to dress up your bear. Maybe make a shirt or a pair of overalls or a skirt.

SUPPLIES

- Egg carton
- Acrylic paint
- Tacky glue or low-temperature glue gun
- Brown foam sheet
- Googly eyes
- Black pom-pom
- Marker

DIRECTIONS

Cut four sections out of an egg carton. Paint them brown and set them aside to dry. Glue two sections together and then do the same thing with the other two sections. Place one of the glued sections upright and then glue the other on top, facing sideways. Cut shapes out of the brown sheet of foam for the ears, arms, and legs. Glue those pieces into place. Glue the googly eyes to the top sections of egg carton and then glue a small pom-pom underneath the eyes to form the nose. Use a marker to draw in small details.

EGG CARTON WATCH

This egg carton watch is great for dress up and pretend play.

SUPPLIES

- Toilet paper roll
- Acrylic paint
- Egg carton
- Marker
- Pipe cleaner
- Split pin
- Tacky glue or a low-temperature glue gun

DIRECTIONS

Cut a piece of toilet paper roll about 1 inch thick. Paint the ring and a section of egg carton in the color or colors of your choice and then set them aside to dry. You will want to paint the center of the egg carton in a separate color for the face. Use a marker to write in your numbers along the outside of the egg carton. Cut your toilet paper ring so that is able to cuff around your wrist. Poke a hole through the center of your egg carton. Cut a small section of pipe cleaner to use as the hands of your watch. Wrap the pipe cleaner around the split pin and insert it into the hole. Glue the egg carton to the middle of the toilet paper roll cuff.

GOOGLY EYE GOGGLES

I don't care what anyone says, googly eyes are just fun, especially the jumbo ones. Make these silly googly eye goggles just for the giggles.

SUPPLIES

- Egg carton
- Acrylic paint
- Large googly eyes in various colors
- Tacky glue
- Bendable straw

DIRECTIONS

Cut an egg carton so that you have two connected end pieces. The end pieces should leave you with an edge along the top. Keep that edge intact. Trim around the opposite side, rounding out the egg carton pieces and cutting off any jagged pieces. Paint your sections however you like. Have fun with it and be creative. Let the paint dry and then glue the googly eyes to the center of each section. Glue or tape a bent straw to the side of your goggles for a handle.

OAT CONTAINER PIGGY BANK

Other containers will work for this as well. Try a bread crumb container or a drink mix one.

SUPPLIES

- Empty oat container
- Pink tissue paper
- School glue
- Pink acrylic paint
- Egg carton
- Low-temperature glue gun
- Pink button
- Googly eyes
- Pink foam sheets
- Pink pipe cleaner
- Craft sticks

DIRECTIONS

Peel the label off the container of oats. Poke a slit into the center of the container. Make the slot large enough that you can fit large coins and bills into it. Tear pink tissue paper into small pieces. Glue the tissue paper pieces all over the container, avoiding the lid. Make sure to keep the slit open. While working with your bank, be sure that the slit is always facing up. Paint the lid and cut five sections of egg carton and paint them in pink. Let them dry. Glue one of the egg carton pieces to the center of the lid with a low-temperature glue gun. Glue a pink button on the center of the egg carton piece to form a snout. Glue on the googly eyes right above the egg carton piece. Cut ears out of the foam and use the glue gun to glue them into place. Curl a pink pipe cleaner and glue to the back of the container. Glue the other four egg carton pieces to the bottom of the bank to form the pig's legs. You can glue jumbo craft sticks below the legs to stabilize the piggy bank.

CARDBOARD ROLL TELESCOPE

Small children may need assistance with some of the steps for this craft. It will make a wonderful prop for pretend play when it is finished. Pair it with the treasure map from the Tissue Paper chapter for pirate play.

SUPPLIES

- Toilet paper tubes
- Paper towel tube
- Acrylic paint
- Paper cup
- Tacky glue or a low-temperature glue gun

DIRECTIONS

Cut two toilet paper tubes in half the long way. Glue them back into a roll, but with the cardboard overlapping a bit so that both tubes are narrower than the paper towel tube and so that one toilet paper tube is narrower than the other. Trim an inch or two off your paper towel tube and set it aside. Paint all three cardboard tubes in the color of your choice. Cut the bottom off a paper cup. Paint it and let it dry. Glue the larger of the two toilet paper rolls into the paper towel roll. You may wrap the leftover piece of paper towel tube around the end of the toilet paper roll to get it closer to the inside surface of the paper towel roll so it fits more snugly. Glue the remaining toilet paper roll into the other toilet paper tube. Glue the bottom end of the paper cup into the end of the paper towel tube. Look through your new spyglass. Ahoy, Mateys!!

RECYCLABLE WIND CHIME

If you have a lot of recyclables, this is a perfect craft to put them to good use.

SUPPLIES

- Acrylic paint
- Toilet paper or paper towel tubes
- Egg carton pieces
- Paper plate
- Hole punch
- Yarn
- Yarn needle

DIRECTIONS

Paint all of your recyclables in different colors. Use a hole punch to poke holes around the outer edges of the toilet paper tubes. Poke holes through the center of your egg carton pieces. Poke holes around the outer and inner edges of the paper plate. String and knot off the yarn through each of the holes. The inner pieces of yarn can be brought up like a tent and tied off at the top for hanging. The outer pieces can be used to string up the painted recyclables. A yarn needle can be used to do this easily.

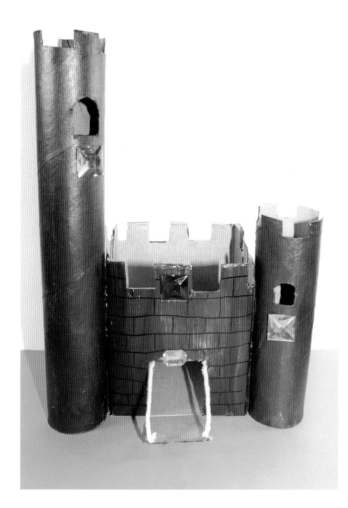

TISSUE BOX CASTLE

Make your castle as big as you want by adding additional tissue boxes and paper towel tube towers. Fill your castle with action figures or brick people.

SUPPLIES

- Tissue box
- Acrylic paint
- Paper towel tube
- Toilet paper tube
- Tacky glue
- Yarn
- Black marker
- Gemstones

DIRECTIONS

Cut the top of the tissue box off so that it is completely open on top. Poke a slit into the bottom half where a door should be and cut a flap that can fold down for the drawbridge. Cut a castle design along the top of the box and then paint the whole box in the color of your choice. Cut little windows out of the paper towel and toilet paper tubes. Paint both tubes. Let them dry. Glue the tubes to either side of the box. Pull the drawbridge flap down and glue small pieces of yarn to the flap and then to the inside of the opening. Use a marker to draw in lines to form bricks on the box. Decorate your castle with gemstones to finish it off.

TOILET PAPER TUBE FAIRY VILLAGE

Mini villages are always fun. If fairies aren't your thing, try making a small city or a farm or try a seasonal village for the holidays.

SUPPLIES

- Toilet paper or paper towel tubes
- Acrylic paint
- Marker
- Mini cupcake liners
- Egg carton pieces
- Tacky glue

DIRECTIONS

To make the fairy houses, cut a cardboard tube to the desired size. Paint the tubes in the colors of your choice and then set aside to dry. Use a marker to draw windows and doors on each house. Glue on a mini cupcake liner for a roof. To form the toadstools, paint a piece of cardboard tube in white and paint a piece of egg carton in red and let it dry. Dot white paint onto the egg carton and let it dry again. Place the egg carton piece over the white roll and glue into place to secure. Form a village with your houses and toadstools.

EGG CARTON CARS

Build roads with pieces of construction paper for your egg carton cars. Use tissue boxes and toilet paper tubes to form buildings and build a whole play city.

SUPPLIES

- Acrylic paint
- Egg carton pieces
- Tacky glue
- Large buttons
- White foam
- Black marker

DIRECTIONS

Paint the egg carton pieces and let them dry. Glue two buttons to each side of each egg carton, gluing four buttons total to each car. Cut a small piece of foam and glue it to the front of the egg carton to form a window. Use a marker to draw in the doors on the side or any other details.

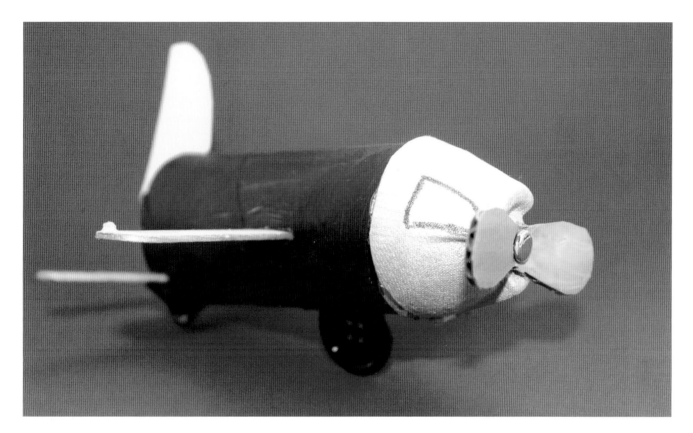

TOILET PAPER TUBE AIRPLANE

Kids love airplanes. This is a cool craft for your airplane lovers.

SUPPLIES

- Egg carton section
- Cardboard
- Toilet paper tube
- Acrylic paint
- Jumbo craft stick
- Regular craft stick
- Split pin
- Low-temperature glue gun
- Buttons (large and small)
- Black marker

DIRECTIONS

Cut one small section of egg carton so that the bottom of the section is cut evenly. Cut a propeller and back fin out of cardboard. Cut slits on each side of the toilet paper tube about one-third of the way down. Cut another slit underneath the tube centered under the two side slits. Paint the egg carton, toilet paper tube, cardboard, and craft sticks in the color or colors of your choosing and set them aside to dry. Poke a hole into the center of the egg carton and the propeller. Insert a split pin into the hole made on the propeller and insert it into the egg carton. Bend the split pin behind the egg carton to hold the pin in place. Glue the egg carton piece to the end of the toilet paper tube on the side closest to the slits. Insert the jumbo craft stick into the side slits on the toilet paper tube. Cut a slit in the top center of the back end of the toilet paper tube. Glue the back fin into the slit. Cut another slit below on both sides of the tube. Glue the smaller craft stick into the slit. Glue the big button into the slit that you cut underneath the front craft stick wing. Cut one last slit into the bottom center of the back end of the tube and glue the small button into it. Use a marker to draw in windows or any other details.

CHAPTER ELEVEN

TISSUE PAPER

Tissue paper can create gorgeous crafts or artwork. You can layer it, crumple it, or make breathtaking stained glass projects with it.

Craft #1: Tissue Paper Artist Palette
Craft #2: Stained Glass Jar
Craft #3: Tissue Paper Acorn
Craft #4: Tissue Paper Apple
Craft #5: Tissue Paper Carrot
Craft #6: Tissue Paper Earth
Craft #7: Tissue Paper Tree
Craft #8: Tissue Paper Fireplace
Craft #9: Tissue Paper Treasure Map
Craft #10: Tissue Paper Ocean Landscape
Craft #11: Tissue Paper Umbrella Suncatcher
Craft #12: Tissue Paper Storm
Craft #13: Tissue Paper Fishbowl
Craft #14: Tissue Paper Peace Sign
Craft #15: Tissue Paper Toucan

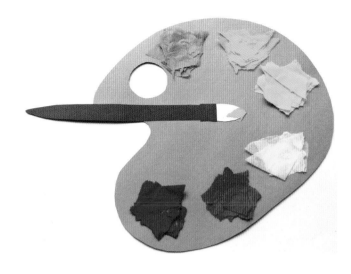

TISSUE PAPER ARTIST PALETTE

Every great artist needs a palette. Create your own colorful palette using pieces of tissue paper.

SUPPLIES
- Brown, white, and black construction paper
- Tissue paper
- Glue stick

DIRECTIONS

Cut out the shape of an artist's palette using a piece of brown construction paper. Tear up tissue paper in a variety of colors into small pieces. We used all the colors of the rainbow. Using just one color of tissue paper, glue and layer it on the outer edge of the palette in a small section similar to a paint splotch. Do this with each color around the palette. Cut a long narrow shape out of a piece of black construction paper to form the brush. Cut a small brush tip out of a piece of white construction paper and then layer a small piece of tissue paper in any color to the end of the brush to form a bit of paint. Glue the brush to the palette.

STAINED GLASS JAR

These are so beautiful either lit or unlit. Use a flameless candle for safety. You can also draw pictures or designs on your jars with a marker to help enhance the stained glass look.

SUPPLIES
- Different colored tissue paper
- Mod Podge
- Glass jar

DIRECTIONS

Cut or tear the pieces of tissue paper and set them aside. Use a paintbrush to brush a thin layer of Mod Podge onto the jar. Place the first layer of tissue paper over the Mod Podge, spreading out the different colors. Brush another layer of Mod Podge over the tissue and overlap over the first layer. Continue to layer the tissue until you are satisfied with the look of your jar.

TISSUE PAPER ACORN

SUPPLIES

- Brown and orange construction paper
- Brown tissue paper
- Glue stick

DIRECTIONS

Draw a picture of a large acorn out of a piece of brown construction paper. Cut off the cap of the acorn. Cut strips of brown tissue paper. Glue the bottom portion of the acorn to the orange construction paper. Use the strips of tissue paper to layer and weave across the top of the acorn. Glue the strips in place and cut any excess tissue off if it sticks out past the acorn cap's shape. Glue the cap above the bottom of the acorn.

TISSUE PAPER APPLE

A is for apple. Apples are a great kid's craft. They can be used for a variety of themes: back to school, autumn, or for lessons on your ABCs.

SUPPLIES

- Construction paper
- Tacky glue
- Red tissue paper

DIRECTIONS

Cut a piece of red construction paper into the shape of an apple. Glue it to the center of another piece of construction paper in any color. Cut a stem and leaves out of the brown and green construction papers and glue them above the apple shape. Tear the red tissue paper into a bunch of small pieces and roll them into little balls and glue them to the apple.

TISSUE PAPER CARROT

This is a simple and quick craft, but you can cover the main part of the carrot in orange tissue paper to add a bit more to your craft.

SUPPLIES

- Orange construction paper
- Green tissue paper
- Tacky glue
- Black marker

DIRECTIONS

Cut a long triangular shape out of a piece of orange construction paper. Cut strips of green tissue paper and glue them to the top of your triangle so that they are sticking out of the top. Twist and bend the tissue pieces. Use a black marker to draw lines on the carrot.

TISSUE PAPER EARTH

You can choose to cover the paper plate in patches of blue instead of painting it. For a more advanced craft, you can crumple up both the blue and green tissue and fill the plate with the crumbled pieces to form your land and sea.

SUPPLIES

- Paper plate
- Blue acrylic paint
- Green tissue paper
- Tacky glue

DIRECTIONS

Paint a paper plate in blue paint and let it dry. Tear and crumple up green tissue paper. Glue the tissue paper around the plate, forming large masses to represent the land. It does not have to be perfect; it will give the effect of the earth, so do not worry too much about making perfect shapes.

TISSUE PAPER TREE

You can make these for any season. Choose green tissue for the summer, pink tissue for spring cherry blossoms, or top with white tissue or pom-poms for winter.

SUPPLIES

- Acrylic paint
- Craft sticks
- Tacky glue
- Tissue paper (red, orange, yellow, or green)

DIRECTIONS

Paint six craft sticks in brown and one in green. Set them aside to dry. Glue two of the brown craft sticks together side by side. Hold them vertically and then glue the green stick perpendicular across the bottom. Spread out the other four craft sticks and glue, fanned out, along the top of the two brown sticks. Tear and crumple up pieces of tissue paper and glue to the four fanned-out sticks.

TISSUE PAPER FIREPLACE

This would also make a great holiday craft by adding stockings to the mantel.

SUPPLIES

- Construction paper
- Black marker
- Glue stick
- Brown acrylic paint
- Craft sticks
- Red, orange, and yellow tissue paper

DIRECTIONS

Cut a large square out of a piece of red construction paper. Cut another medium-sized square out of the bottom center of that same piece of paper to form your fireplace shape. Use a marker to draw brick lines across the fireplace. Glue your fireplace over a larger square shape to form a mantel and the sides of your fireplace. Paint two craft sticks in brown and let them dry. Glue the craft sticks to the inside of the fireplace, crisscrossed. Cut flame shapes out of your different colored tissue papers and glue them over your craft sticks.

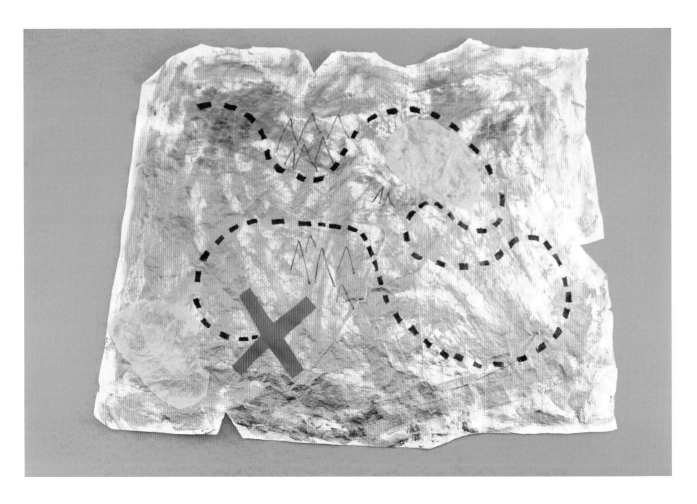

TISSUE PAPER TREASURE MAP

Add an extra element of fun and hide some treasure throughout your home or outside.

SUPPLIES

- Tissue paper
- Bronze paint
- Glue stick
- Thick black marker
- Thick brown marker
- Thick green marker

DIRECTIONS

Roughly cut a large rectangle out of the tissue paper. Cut a few randomly placed "V"-shaped notches out of the sides of the rectangle. Use a piece of tissue to blot on the bronze paint to add an old look to the paper. Cut an "X" out of the red tissue paper and glue it onto the map. Cut kidney and oval shapes out of the blue tissue and glue around the map to represent bodies of water. Use the black marker to draw dashes around the map, circling around the bodies of water and leading to the "X." Use the brown and green markers to draw in simple trees around the mountains on the map.

TISSUE PAPER OCEAN LANDSCAPE

You may choose any kind of simple landscape for this. Try a mountain scene or a forest.

SUPPLIES

- Tissue paper (shades of brown, blue, yellow, white, and orange)
- Glue stick
- Construction paper
- Markers

DIRECTIONS

Tear strips of tissue paper in each of the colors; tear long strips, short, straight, and wavy. Starting from the bottom up, place and glue down a mixture of shades of brown tissue on the bottom one-third of your paper. Overlap the pieces. Glue different shades of dark blue tissue to the middle third. Glue lighter shades of blue tissue to the upper third of the paper. On the top third, add layers of white tissue to form clouds and short strips of yellow and orange tissue for the sunset. Use a marker to add small details to some of the strips.

TISSUE PAPER UMBRELLA SUNCATCHER

The transparency of the tissue paper gives off a great effect when in the sun.

SUPPLIES

- Paper plate
- Black acrylic paint
- Glue
- Wax paper
- Tissue paper
- Construction paper

DIRECTIONS

Cut an umbrella shape out of a paper plate. Cut into the center of your shape and cut a smaller umbrella shape out of the inside. Paint the shape in black paint and let it dry. Use the leftover piece of paper plate and cut out four strips to put inside of the umbrella shape. Paint them black as well and then let them dry. Glue the strips to the back of the plate so that it makes segments in your umbrella, as shown. Cut a piece of wax paper and glue or tape it to the back. Make sure to trim off any excess overhanging paper. Tear assorted colors of tissue paper and glue them to the back of the umbrella onto the wax paper. Cut a handle out of construction paper and glue it to the bottom of the umbrella.

TISSUE PAPER STORM

As an alternative to this, you may also layer bleeding tissue paper and instead of gluing it down, spray it with water to get a watercolor effect as your base.

SUPPLIES

- Tissue paper (black and blue)
- Glue stick
- Construction paper (white, blue, and yellow)

DIRECTIONS

Tear the blue and black tissue paper into small pieces. Run the glue stick over a piece of white construction paper, working in small sections, and glue the black and blue tissue onto the white construction paper. Add more glue as needed and layer on more tissue paper. Cut raindrops out of the blue construction paper and cut a lightning bolt out of a piece of yellow construction paper and glue onto your tissue paper backdrop.

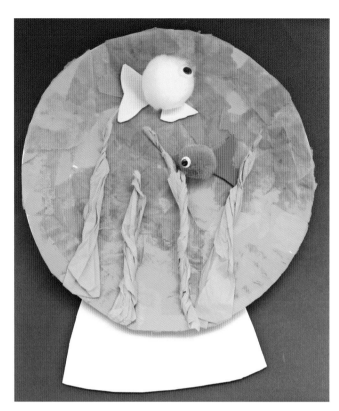

TISSUE PAPER FISHBOWL

Use paint or markers to add in other elements to your fishbowl. Make more fish or an underwater castle.

SUPPLIES

- Blue and green tissue paper
- Paper plate
- Construction paper (any color)
- Tacky glue
- Googly eyes
- Craft pom-poms

DIRECTIONS

Tear off pieces of blue tissue paper. Cover a paper plate in the blue tissue. Twist pieces of green tissue paper to make underwater plant life and glue them to the bottom of the plate. Cut the base of your fishbowl out of a piece of construction paper and glue it into place. To form a fish, glue a googly eye to a craft pom-pom. Cut fins out of construction paper and glue them to the pom-pom, as well.

TISSUE PAPER PEACE SIGN

Another great alternative is to use bleeding tissue paper and water to create a beautiful watercolor painted look on your peace sign. See this technique used in the Tissue Paper Bleeding Heart craft.

SUPPLIES

- Paper plate
- Tissue paper
- Glue stick

DIRECTIONS

Cut a peace sign shape out of a paper plate. Tear up different colored tissue paper into small pieces. Run the glue stick over the plate, working in small sections, and cover the glue with tissue paper. Add more glue as needed and overlap with more paper. Fold and glue the excess tissue under the plate or trim off the excess overhanging tissue paper.

TISSUE PAPER TOUCAN

It's all about the beak in this one. Toucan beaks are so bright and colorful. You can choose to glue the strips down and make rows of different colors, or you can crumple up the tissue into little balls and glue in colorful rows.

SUPPLIES

- Black, white, and green construction paper
- Glue stick
- Tissue paper (rainbow colors)
- Large googly eye
- Black marker

DIRECTIONS

Cut a large oval out of a piece of black construction paper. Hold a piece of green construction paper in landscape position. Glue the oval close to one of the sides of the green construction paper to form the body of your toucan. Cut a tail out of the black construction paper and then glue it to the bottom of the oval. Cut a large beak shape out of a piece of white construction paper. Tear pieces of tissue paper out of each color. Glue and layer the tissue paper in rows. Add a large googly eye to the top of the body near the beak. Draw little feet onto the bottom of your toucan to finish him off.

CHAPTER TWELVE

YARN

Yarn crafts are excellent for building fine motor skills and concentration. Whether you are yarn wrapping or trying to cut or coil it, these yarn activities demand focus from your child.

Craft #1: Mustache & Beard Masks

Craft #2: Dream Catchers

Craft #3: Make Your Own Pizza

Craft #4: Shape Yarn Sewing

Craft #5: Spider Web

Craft #6: Yarn Bird's Nest

Craft #7: Yarn Cactus

Craft #8: Yarn Cow

Craft #9: Yarn Dolls

Craft #10: Yarn Skunk

Craft #11: Yarn Snail

Craft #12: Yarn-Wrapped Bongos

Craft #13: Yarn-Wrapped Heart

Craft #14: Yarn-Wrapped Initial

Craft #15: Yarn-Wrapped Strawberry

MUSTACHE & BEARD MASKS

These are loads of silly fun to make and to play with after. Make them in all different shapes and colors. These would be a great party prop, as well.

SUPPLIES

- Cardboard
- Tacky glue
- Craft stick
- Yarn

DIRECTIONS

Cut a mustache and/or beard shape out of cardboard. Glue a craft stick to the back of it. Cover the cardboard in glue and cut strands of yarn to make the hair for the mustache and the beard. Curl pieces of yarn around your fingers to make curls or just glue straight for straight hair.

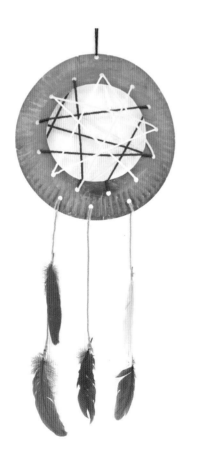

DREAM CATCHERS

SUPPLIES

- Paper plate
- Acrylic paint
- Hole punch
- Different colored yarn
- Feathers

DIRECTIONS

Cut out the center of a paper plate. Paint the remaining ring of the paper plate in the color of your choice and then let it dry. Use a hole punch and punch holes around the inside of the paper plate. String the yarn from hole to hole. Punch a few holes along the bottom outer edge of the plate and then tie strands of yarn down from each of these holes. Tie feathers and beads or other embellishments of your choice to the dangling yarn. Punch a hole at the top and string another piece of yarn through it to hang.

MAKE YOUR OWN PIZZA

This is a fun activity for your pretend chefs. Play pizza parlor and set up a whole work station of pretend toppings.

SUPPLIES

- Construction paper (light brown and red)
- Yellow yarn
- Tacky glue

DIRECTIONS

Cut a circle out of a piece of brown construction paper. Cut a wavy circle for the sauce out of a piece of red construction paper and then glue it to the top of the brown circle. Cut short strands of yellow yarn to use as the cheese and then glue the yarn cheese to the top of the pizza. Cut out pepperoni circles or crumple up small pieces of brown construction paper for the hamburger mushrooms. Use construction paper or foam to cut out any other toppings of your choice.

SHAPE YARN SEWING

This is a wonderful fine motor activity for the kids and a fun way to learn how to sew. Another fun alternative is to cut a bunch of square pieces and sew a foam quilt.

SUPPLIES

- Foam sheets
- Hole punch
- Yarn needle
- Yarn

DIRECTIONS

Cut assorted shapes out of different colored foam sheets. Use a hole punch to punch holes around the outside of each shape. Thread a yarn needle with yarn and tie a knot at the bottom. Insert into one of the holes and practice sewing around each shape.

SPIDER WEB

This is a great introduction to yarn-wrapped crafts. Let a little yarn dangle off of your web and tie another spider to the end.

SUPPLIES

- Paper plate
- White yarn
- Black pipe cleaner
- Tacky glue
- Large pom-pom
- Googly eyes

DIRECTIONS

Cut out the center of a paper plate. Cut slits around the outside of the plate. Loop the yarn around the plate, catching it in the grooves. To form the spider: cut two pipe cleaners in half to form four smaller pieces. Bend the pipe cleaners and glue them under a large pom-pom to form eight legs. Glue the googly eyes to the pom-pom and let the glue dry. Insert your spider onto its web.

YARN BIRD'S NEST

Birds' nests are usually made up of all sorts of materials. Combine a few nature elements to your nest, such as small twigs or leaves.

SUPPLIES

- Paper plate
- Brown, yellow, and white yarn
- Tacky glue
- Construction paper
- Googly eyes
- Optional: feathers

DIRECTIONS

Cut a paper plate in half. Cut small strands out of brown, yellow, or white yarn. Glue the yarn all over the plate. Cut a couple of bird shapes out of construction paper in any color and glue beaks onto the birds. Add googly eyes to your birds. For a little added fun, glue on some feathers.

YARN CACTUS

You don't have to worry about pricking yourself on this cactus. The needles here are soft.

SUPPLIES

- Brown and green construction paper
- Brown yarn

DIRECTIONS

Cut a cactus shape out of a piece of green construction paper. Glue the shape to a piece of brown construction paper. Cut a bunch of small pieces of brown yarn. Glue the pieces to the outer edges of the cactus as if they were needles.

YARN COW

You can coil your yarn into a perfect oval shape or loosely glue your yarn wildly to make your cow's head.

SUPPLIES

- Construction paper
- White and black yarn
- School glue
- Jumbo googly eyes
- Large black buttons
- Black marker

DIRECTIONS

Draw a large half circle lightly with a pencil at the top of a piece of construction paper. Cut a large pink oval out of construction paper and glue it under your half circle sketch. Cut strands of white and black yarn. Spread glue around the half circle and spread the strands of yarn around inside the half circle. Add more glue and keep adding yarn until you have filled in your cow's face as much as you would like. Coil pieces of black yarn around your finger to form spots and then glue them onto the white. Glue the jumbo-sized googly eyes onto the yarn. Cut ears and horns out of white or black construction paper and then glue them to the head. Glue two large buttons onto the upper left and right ends of the pink oval to form nostrils. Draw a mouth onto your cow to finish him off.

YARN DOLLS

To make this simpler for smaller children, you can forgo the arms and legs and just wrap the craft stick with the yarn.

SUPPLIES

- Craft sticks (jumbo and regular)
- Low-temperature glue gun or tacky glue
- Different colored yarn
- Googly eyes
- Markers
- Buttons

DIRECTIONS

To form the boy, break two regular-sized craft sticks in half. This will give you four pieces. Glue two of the small pieces to the bottom of a jumbo stick to form legs and then glue two to the side to form arms. For the girl, break two regular-sized sticks in half again. Use three of the halves to form a triangle and then glue it to a jumbo stick about halfway down. Break another regular stick in half and use it for the arms. Begin wrapping your dolls with yarn right above the arms and work your way down. Use different colored yarn or all the same color. Wrap around the arms and legs or skirt if you made a skirt. Tie a knot when you are done wrapping or add a bit of glue at the end to hold your yarn in place. Leave the section above the arms uncovered for the head. Glue googly eyes onto your dolls and draw in any facial features with markers. Cut pieces of yarn for the hair. Add buttons or other embellishments to your bodies to dress up your dolls a bit.

YARN SKUNK

They may be little stinkers, but they still are pretty cute.

SUPPLIES

- Black and white construction paper
- School glue
- Pink pom-pom
- Googly eye
- White yarn

DIRECTIONS

Cut a large oval shape and a smaller circle out of a piece of black construction paper for the body and the head. Cut a small triangle for the nose and four small rectangles for the legs also out of the black construction paper. Cut a large curvy shape for the tail and a small half oval for the ear. Glue the large oval shape to the center of a piece of white construction paper for the skunk's body. Glue the circle at a slant to the upper side of the oval to form the head. Glue the triangle to the circle for the nose and then glue the four rectangles below the oval-shaped body to form the legs. Glue the tail and ear in place. Glue a pink pom-pom to the end of the nose and add on the googly eye. Cut strands of white yarn and glue along the top of the head, body, and the tail to form the white streak on the skunk.

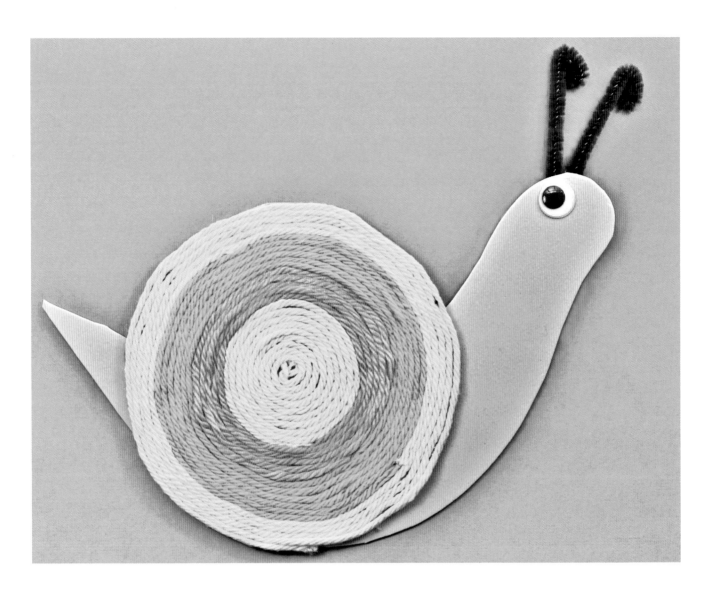

YARN SNAIL

Coiling the yarn for this project is a wonderful fine motor activity. This may be a little tricky for the smaller kids, but it will be great practice.

SUPPLIES

- Cardboard
- Tacky glue
- Yarn in various colors
- Foam sheets
- Googly eye

DIRECTIONS

Cut a large circle out of a piece of cardboard. Cover the cardboard in glue and coil the yarn on top of the cardboard in a circular pattern. Cut a piece of foam sheet to form the head and the tail of the snail. Glue the foam head and tail to the yarn-covered body. Glue a googly eye to the head to finish it off.

YARN-WRAPPED BONGOS

Wrap your bongos and then pair them up with your glittery maracas from the All That Glitters chapter.

SUPPLIES

- Empty oat containers
- Acrylic paint
- Yarn
- Tacky glue or low-temperature glue gun
- Foam pieces
- Pipe cleaners

DIRECTIONS

Clean out the inside of two containers and peel off the outside label. Paint the containers in the color or colors of your choice and let them dry. Wrap the top or bottom half of each container with yarn. Glue the ends when you have wrapped all that you want. Wrap another piece of yarn around both containers a few times to join them together and then wrap another piece of yarn around the yarn between both containers. Cut zigzag shapes out of the foam and glue around your bongos. Cut triangle shapes out of the foam and then cut small pieces of pipe cleaner. Glue the pieces to the top side of the drum to form the top clamps around the drums.

YARN-WRAPPED HEART

Yarn wrapping is a great exercise to flex those fine motor muscles.

SUPPLIES

- Cardboard
- Acrylic paint
- Yarn in various colors

DIRECTIONS

Cut a large heart out of cardboard. Cut another heart shape out of the center. Paint both sides of your heart with acrylic paint in the color of your choice. Set it aside to let it dry. Cut long strands of yarn. Wrap the pieces of yarn around the heart, working through the center and around the outside. When you are finished, tie a knot at the end or use a little bit of glue to hold it into place.

YARN-WRAPPED INITIAL

Do just an initial or try to wrap your full name. This is a great project for your child to display in their room.

SUPPLIES

- Tacky glue or low-temperature glue gun
- Craft sticks
- Acrylic paint
- Different colored yarn

DIRECTIONS

Overlap and glue the craft sticks to form a square letter of your choosing. Let the glue dry. Paint your letter and then set it aside to dry. Cut long strands of yarn. Wrap the painted letter with the strands of yarn. Tie it off and knot it at the end when you are finished or glue it into place.

YARN-WRAPPED STRAWBERRY

Make a whole collection of yarn-wrapped fruits using simple cardboard shapes. A yarn-wrapped orange and banana would be fun to make, too.

SUPPLIES

- Cardboard
- Red acrylic paint
- Red yarn
- Green foam sheets

DIRECTIONS

Cut a piece of cardboard into a strawberry shape. Paint the cardboard in red and set it aside to dry. Cut small notches around the edge of the strawberry. Wrap the yarn around the notches. Continue to wrap the strawberry. There is no need to wrap the whole thing. When you have achieved your desired look, tie off the yarn in the back and knot it or use a little bit of glue to hold it in place. Cut a stem and leaves out of a piece of green foam and then glue them into place.

CHAPTER THIRTEEN

SEASONS AND HOLIDAYS

What better way for the kids to get into the spirit of the holidays than with some holiday-inspired crafts.

Craft #1: Button Candy Cane

Craft #2: Craft Stick Christmas Tree

Craft #3: Cupcake Liner Pot of Gold

Craft #4: Paper Plate Easter Bonnet

Craft #5: Fourth of July Sequin Fireworks Painting

Craft #6: Button Flag Craft

Craft #7: Ghost Window

Craft #8: Mother's and Father's Day Thumprint Craft

Craft #9: Stained Glass Pumpkin

Craft #10: Painted Snowflakes

Craft #11: Tissue Paper Bleeding Heart

Craft #12: Paper Fan Turkey

Craft #13: Tissue Box Santa Stuck in the Chimney

Craft #14: Washi Tape Easter Eggs

Craft #15: Handprint Bat

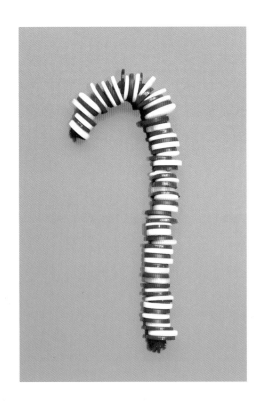

BUTTON CANDY CANE

Besides being a great way to practice fine motor skills, the alternating from red to white is great for learning patterns.

SUPPLIES

- White pipe cleaner
- Red and white buttons

DIRECTIONS

Bend one end of the pipe cleaner slightly so that buttons wont slide off. String buttons onto the pipe cleaner on the unbent side, alternating red and white buttons. Once the pipe cleaner is full, bend the pipe cleaner on the other end to hold the buttons in place on the opposite end, as well. Curve the pipe cleaner into a candy cane shape.

CRAFT STICK CHRISTMAS TREE

Who doesn't love decorating a Christmas tree? Here is a wonderful opportunity to decorate as many Christmas trees as you like and with no risk of breaking any bulbs.

SUPPLIES

- Craft sticks
- Green acrylic paint
- Tacky glue
- Green and brown construction paper
- Buttons, sequins, gemstones, or glitter

DIRECTIONS

Paint the craft sticks in green paint and let them dry. Glue the three sticks together to form a triangle. Cut a triangle out of a piece of green construction paper in roughly the same size. Glue the paper to the back of the triangle. Cut a small rectangle out of a piece of brown construction paper for the tree trunk and glue it to the bottom center of your triangle. Decorate your tree with buttons, gemstones, sequins, or glitter.

CUPCAKE LINER POT OF GOLD

You don't need to wait for a rainbow to discover a pot of gold; all you need are some cupcake liners and construction paper. This is an adorable craft for St. Patrick's Day.

SUPPLIES

- Black and white construction paper
- Construction paper in rainbow colors
- Gold or yellow mini cupcake liners

DIRECTIONS

Cut a pot out of a piece of black construction paper. Cut strips out of construction paper in each color of the rainbow. Fan out the rainbow strips and glue them to a sheet of white construction paper. Glue the pot onto the bottom center of the paper. Flatten out your cupcake liners and glue them to the top of the pot. Fill your pot up with as much gold as you would like.

PAPER PLATE EASTER BONNET

This is a fun craft to make with the added bonus of being able to wear it on your head afterward.

SUPPLIES

- Tacky glue
- Paper or Styrofoam bowl
- Paper plate
- Acrylic paint
- Ribbon
- Foam or plastic flowers

DIRECTIONS

Glue your bowl to the top of the paper plate. Once the glue is dry, paint the bowl and plate in the color of your choice. Let the paint dry and cut a piece of ribbon to go around your bonnet. (Cloth unwired ribbon works the best.) Glue foam or plastic flowers around the hat to dress it up.

Kim Uliana   157

FOURTH OF JULY SEQUIN FIREWORKS PAINTING

This is full of sparkle and festive fun.

SUPPLIES

- Acrylic or tempura paint
- Watercolor paper
- School glue
- Sequins

DIRECTIONS

Start by painting a piece of watercolor paper in black, or if you'd like, start on a piece of thick black stock paper. Paint different colored circles around your paper with lines coming out from inside of the circles and bursting out all around them. Glue sequins around your painting once it is dry to add a festive touch.

BUTTON FLAG CRAFT

Instead of buttons, you may also consider using paint and fingerprints or Q-tips for a different idea or ball up small pieces of white tissue or paper to form your stars.

SUPPLIES

- Red, white, and blue construction paper
- Tacky glue
- White buttons

DIRECTIONS

Cut or tear long strips of red construction paper for your flag stripes and then glue them to a piece of white construction paper, evenly spacing out each strip. Cut or tear a blue square from a piece of blue construction paper and glue to the upper-left-hand corner of your stripes. Glue white buttons to your blue square to form the stars.

GHOST WINDOW

Make different haunted windows. Make spooky eyes, bats, or a jack-o-lantern peeking out behind your window.

SUPPLIES

- Craft sticks
- Black acrylic paint
- White and black construction paper
- Tacky glue
- Googly eyes
- Optional: black button

DIRECTIONS

Paint six craft sticks in black paint and set them aside to let them dry. Cut a simple ghost shape out of white construction paper. Glue four of the painted craft sticks to form a square and then glue one craft stick through the center front vertically and then the last craft stick through the center back horizontally. Cut a square of black construction paper that will fit behind your frame. Glue your ghost shape to the black paper and glue your frame over the ghost square. Glue your googly eyes to the ghost and add a button for the mouth or use a marker or a round piece of construction paper instead.

MOTHER'S AND FATHER'S DAY THUMBPRINT CRAFT

This is a lovely keepsake to hang in your house. You can make one of just the kids or the whole family. This would also be a wonderful gift for the grandparents.

SUPPLIES

- Rolling pin
- Air dry clay
- Cookie cutter
- Drinking straw
- Acrylic paint
- Black marker
- Yarn

DIRECTIONS

Use a rolling pin to roll out a clump of clay. Use a cookie cutter or free form a shape large enough to fit the thumbprints on. Press a straw into the top of your shape to form a hole to put a string through. Press each thumb into the clay close together. Let the clay dry. It might take a day or two. Paint the dry clay in the color of your choice and paint each thumbprint in a different color. Let the paint dry. Use a marker to draw in faces. Draw in stick arms and hands and have your thumbprints holding hands. Tie a piece of yarn through the hole at the top.

STAINED GLASS PUMPKIN

Tissue paper creates a beautiful stained glass look that is perfect for holiday crafts.

SUPPLIES

- Paper plate
- Orange paint
- Wax paper
- Orange and yellow tissue paper
- Green construction paper
- Green pipe cleaners
- Tacky glue, tape, or staples

DIRECTIONS

Cut three crescent-shaped slices out of the inside of a paper plate. Paint the bottom part of the paper plate in orange paint and let it dry. Flip the plate around once it is dry and glue a round piece of wax paper to the unpainted side. Glue and layer orange and yellow tissue paper to the wax paper covering the circle. Cut a piece of green construction paper to form the stem and then glue it to the top of the plate. Curl a couple of pipe cleaners and staple, tape, or glue them into place. Pipe cleaners can be tricky to glue, so the staples or tape might work best.

PAINTED SNOWFLAKES

This is a wonderful process art project. Any paint will do for this. There are no rules, just paint.

SUPPLIES

- White paper
- Watercolors, tempura, or acrylic paints

DIRECTIONS

Paint a sheet of paper with the paints of your choice. Let the paint dry and then cut into a snowflake.

TISSUE PAPER BLEEDING HEART

If you have not tried bleeding tissue paper yet, you should. It is fun to work with and leaves a soft watercolor effect.

SUPPLIES

- Watercolor paper
- Bleeding tissue paper
- Spray bottle
- Water

DIRECTIONS

Draw a heart shape onto a piece of watercolor paper. Tear up pieces of bleeding tissue paper in reds and pinks and place them within your heart shape, overlapping the colors. Fill a spray bottle with water and spray the pieces of tissue. Let the tissue sit and dry. When the paper dries, remove the tissue to reveal the bled color.

PAPER FAN TURKEY

This technique can work for a number of animals. Fan it out into a full circle for even more alternatives.

SUPPLIES

- Acrylic paint
- Construction paper
- Tacky glue
- Craft stick
- Googly eyes

DIRECTIONS

Paint stripes of dark brown and black on the top and bottom edge of a piece of light brown construction paper. Let it dry. Form a paper fan with the painted paper. Dab a little glue throughout your fan to hold it in place. Glue a craft stick underneath the fan to keep it upright. Cut a bowling pin shape out of light brown paper to form the turkey's body. Glue googly eyes onto the body. Cut an orange beak and a red waddle out of construction paper and then glue it to the turkey's body. Let the glue dry. Glue the body to the front of the fan.

TISSUE BOX SANTA STUCK IN THE CHIMNEY

This is adorable and is sure to crack your kids up.

SUPPLIES

- Tissue box
- Acrylic paint
- Toilet paper tubes
- Markers
- Tacky glue or low-temperature glue gun
- Cotton balls
- Black foam

DIRECTIONS

Paint a tissue box in red paint and let it dry. Paint two toilet paper tubes three quarters of the way in red paint and then one quarter in black. Let it dry. With a black marker, draw a brick pattern around the painted tissue box. Drizzle glue along the top of the box and spread out a couple of cotton balls. Glue a ring of cotton around a toilet paper tube where the black and the red meet. Cut two ovals out of black foam and glue them to the black painted end to form the boots. Stick the two tubes into the top of the box with the boot side up. Form the tubes into a "V" shape and add a little glue if needed to hold the tubes in place.

WASHI TAPE EASTER EGGS

Washi Tape is a colorful and easy way to add beauty to any craft project; not to mention, the kids love to play with it.

SUPPLIES

- Construction paper
- Washi Tape

DIRECTIONS

Cut the construction paper into egg shapes. Tear off different designs of Washi Tape and place the strips across the egg shapes to decorate your Easter eggs. Cut the excess Washi Tape off the edges.

HANDPRINT BAT

Hand and footprint crafts are always fun and make wonderful keepsakes.

SUPPLIES

- Black, white, and pink construction paper
- Tacky glue
- Googly eyes

DIRECTIONS

Trace both hands onto a piece of black construction paper and cut them out. You may also dip your hands in paint and stamp with your hands for an alternative. Cut an oval shape for the bat's head, two small rectangles for the legs, and two triangles for the ears. Cut smaller triangles out of pink construction paper and glue them inside the black triangles to form ears. Cut two white triangles out of white paper and glue them to the bat's head to form fangs. Glue googly eyes to the bat's head to finish it off.

NOTES